Corpus III

Series Board

James Bernauer

Drucilla Cornell

Thomas R. Flynn

Kevin Hart

Richard Kearney

Jean-Luc Marion

Adriaan Peperzak

Thomas Sheehan

Hent de Vries

Merold Westphal

Michael Zimmerman

John D. Caputo, *series editor*

PERSPECTIVES IN
CONTINENTAL
PHILOSOPHY

JEAN-LUC NANCY

*Translated by Jeff Fort, Agnès Jacob,
Robert St. Clair, Marie-Eve Morin,
and Travis Holloway*

Corpus III
Cruor *and Other Writings*

FORDHAM UNIVERSITY PRESS
New York ▪ 2023

Copyright © 2023 Fordham University Press

All rights reserved. No part of this publication may be reproduced, stored in a retrieval system, or transmitted in any form or by any means—electronic, mechanical, photocopy, recording, or any other—except for brief quotations in printed reviews, without the prior permission of the publisher.

Part I of this book was originally published in French as Jean-Luc Nancy, *Cruor, Suivi de Nostalgie du père*, Copyright © 2021 Éditions Galilée.

Fordham University Press has no responsibility for the persistence or accuracy of URLs for external or third-party Internet websites referred to in this publication and does not guarantee that any content on such websites is, or will remain, accurate or appropriate.

Fordham University Press also publishes its books in a variety of electronic formats. Some content that appears in print may not be available in electronic books.

Visit us online at www.fordhampress.com.

Library of Congress Cataloging-in-Publication Data available online at https://catalog.loc.gov.

Printed in the United States of America

25 24 23   5 4 3 2 1

First edition

Contents

PART I: CRUOR, WITH LONGING FOR THE FATHER

Introduction   *3*

Cruor   *7*

1. Drive (*Pulsion*), 7 • 2. Rhythm, 8 • 3. Self (*Soi*), 9 • 4. You (*Toi*), 11 • 5. *Instance*, 13 • 6. Glorious Body, 15 • 7. Matrix, 17 • 8. It/Self (Erudite Interlude), 19 • 9. Extension, 21 • 10. Self/Same, 22 • 11. Excitation, 24 • 12. For, 25 • 13. Myth, 26 • 14. Sacrifice, 29 • 15. Torture, 31 • 16. Embrace, 33 • 17. Justice, 35 • 18. Sublime, 36 • 19. But Still Again, 37 • 20. Life Is Cruel, 38 • 21. Eros, Thanatos, Cosmos, 39 • 22. Drives without Objects, 41

Longing for the Father   *45*

Lesson   *58*

PART II: STOMA

Hymne Stomique / Stoma: A Hymn   *62*

***Afterword to* Stoma**, by Andrea Gyenge and John Paul Ricco   *97*

PART III: SCANDALOUS DEATH   *109*

Notes   *117*

PART I

Cruor, with Longing for the Father

> And this age wants to be called by
> This terrible Latin word *cruor*
> Which means blood spilled.
>
> —**Guillaume Apollinaire**
> *Couleur du temps* (1918)
> act I, scene 4

Introduction

In 1992 a book appeared under the title *Corpus*.¹ It was republished in 2002 and in 2006 with a few additions that did not substantially modify its content. My concern there was with the extension of the body, or the body as extension: with what makes it an *ex-peausition* (ex-posure-(as/of)-skin), as I wrote it there.² Space-time, the grappling of bodies or the body-to-body [*le corps-à-corps*], contact, all the ways of being outside and, even more, of being an outside.

The initial text of *Corpus* ended with the "between-bodies." It said: "This is how bodies are offered to one another [*entre eux*]," and it disseminated this offering across "a whole corpus of images stretched from body to body, local colors and shadows, fragments, grains, areolas, lunules, nails, hairs, tendons, skulls, ribs, pelvises, bellies, meatuses, foams, tears, teeth, droolings, slits, blocks, tongues, sweat, liquors, veins, pains and joys, and me, and you" (*Corpus*, 121).

In a single leap, "me and you" allowed a transition from the interval or between-two to the between-us, without any preparation for this leap: it seemed necessary, long after, to account for the *between* insofar as it stretches from one body to others, even as it stretches and tenses within each one something like its own drive, which is what makes it a body and makes each and all of us body-to-body.

The body-to-body implies both violence and reserve, the grip of embrace, suffocation, essential ambivalence. In horseback riding, mounting without a saddle is called, in French, "*monter à cru*," literally "riding raw."

One does without any mediation or elaboration of the relation between rider and horse. In the *cru*, the "raw," there is a form and a force of refusal of the "between." Now it seems that our world is set on eliminating every mediation—between human beings and between all the elements of what we used to call "nature." We are faced with the necessity of considering this "raw," this invention of a beyond of mediations in the auto-mediation of a single machine (technical, economic, ethical, and aesthetic). "*L'art cru*" or "raw art" is an artistic and (already) a museum category. Crudeness (of thoughts, of speech), as well as cruelty (of individual or collective acts), is taking over all the spaces of the "between." There is thus a necessity of thinking what up to now seemed relegated to a (repulsive) margin of civilization.[3]

This feeling of necessity is nourished by an increase of various forms of violence throughout the world. Sociologists continue to debate the real or perceived evolutions of violence since the beginning of the twentieth century. These considerations are secondary with respect to a more important element, in which the real and its perception cannot be separated: the absence of legitimation that is affecting our world.

Every civilization possesses its forms of legitimation—sacred, mythic, ideal, fantasmatic, symbolic. Ours is legitimated through and through by technoscientific rationality, from which all legitimacy is presumed to be formed in accordance with its own. From here another question immediately arises: can there be a legitimacy that would derive only from itself?

For the moment, what we are witnessing is rather an auto-destruction than an auto-foundation.

Leonardo da Vinci—of whom we will speak again for other reasons—is one of the most remarkable figures of rational technical humanist inventiveness. It is not by chance that he also bears witness to a consciousness of imminent disorder and distraction, as when he writes, under the title "Of the Cruelty of Men": "Creatures shall be seen on the earth who will always be fighting one with another, with the greatest losses and frequent deaths on either side. There will be no bounds to their malice; by their strong limbs a great portion of the trees in the vast forests of the world shall be laid low; and when they are filled with food the gratification of their desire shall be to deal out death, affliction, labour, terror, and banishment to every living thing."[4]

The question of the "legitimacy of the modern age" is not new.[5] But it was visibly transformed or altered with the effacement of what constituted, under the name of "progress," a potential legitimacy in the strongest sense of the word. For what became dubious was not only the effects of technical progress but also the possibility that another perspective (moral, religious, ideological) could be added to it, opposed to it, or substituted for it. Along with progress, it was also the project in general that crossed a threshold. The project and every kind of projection, if one can indeed distinguish these from technological prefigurations or preemptions.

At the same time (in fact, the time since the collapse of communism, that is, of the political, historical, and theoretical significations brought together in this word), numerous philosophical and psychoanalytical interests in the "death drive" and in "cruelty" have developed, as though out of necessity.[6] The effacement of every project made more visible certain kinds of suffering that no projected expectation could sustain any longer. (One could say: the true end of sacrifice was reached.) Not only wars, guerrilla struggles, and murderous attacks but also violent seizures of power, crushed rebellions, squelched uprisings, everywhere prisons and torture, flight, refugees, famines, emergencies, displaced peoples—along with drugs, addictions, and overdoses—pile up in a mess, forming a general picture of distress in which the torments caused by climate disruption have begun to intensify, along with disruptions in agriculture, medicine, and energy. Statistics show that life expectancy has increased, and that violence has decreased over the course of centuries, but what cannot be measured is the pervasive pain and grief, the confusion and disarray. Art has received from this some surprising shocks. Religions have reacted only by making themselves more compassionate or more culpabilizing, more vacuous or more cruel.

It was not by chance that the project in its most popular form was called "communism." Communism claimed to speak of bodies among and between themselves, of a body-to-body that at the same time would be removed from confrontation and from social totalization. In sum it truly spoke of bodies, of existences that are neither abstract, nor juridical, nor functional, bodies that are the ongoing life of existence. In this respect, one can say that Sartre will have represented the greatest sensitivity to this truth of communism. But history did away with this sensitivity. There remained only political schemas whereas it was a question of much more . . .

With the effacement of communism this sense of bodies (which seemed also, to Marx and later to others, to have been able to exist in older forms of community) was also effaced, or at least blurred. All the questions of the "other [*autrui*]," of the "with" and of the "common" arose again just as the sensitivity I am speaking of was losing its means of expression: the major loss was that of the word "communism," and with it the entire lexicon of community (which Nazism, not at all by chance, had thrown together in a mythological mishmash).

"Living together" and "community relations" became the expressions of a penury in the sense for the common. Dull, vague, and equivocal expressions in which the "together" speaks less of bodies than of societies and institutions. Bodies *touch*,[7] they feel and feel each other (see and hear . . .). Bodies press together and disperse, they clash, stroke, wound, or caress each other. It is not simply "together," it is in constant approach and recoil, it is in contact, in collision, in contagion and constraint, in com-passion— in an unheard-of sense of this word.

That is why "me and you" (the conclusion of *Corpus*) has in thirty years crossed a threshold that made it necessary not to end there but to set out from there once again. Me and you: self and self, how does this [*ça*] happen? It is from here that this continuation of that book emerged.

—Translated by Jeff Fort

Cruor

Not to know, not for anything; something like the blow of a wing, like an ebbing back, a moan of love, and then now, and then maybe, and then yes.[1]

1. Drive (*Pulsion*)[2]

Indeed blood flows and its flow is what makes life and death, the passage from one to the other. We could imagine other ways for this to happen, to transmit to an entire body what it needs. But this is how it is: aside from messages sent through the nerves, it is blood that transports substances of every nature. There is information, and there is metabolism. There are actions and reactions, there are passageways, and there are assimilations and excretions. To simplify, one could say: behaviors and maintenance.

Or else: the relation to the world and the relation to self. Of course, these cannot be unknown to each other or even separated without remainder. If necessary blood can even make up for deficiencies in nervous activity and transmit information. But it is there first of all to carry out maintenance, to absorb air, water, and the rest, to expel waste from them. Thus it does not know sleep, unlike other tissues. Its circulation must not be interrupted.

A pulsing organ is dedicated to this function. The beating of the heart gives the cadence of life itself. Life lives at each instant, in each new pulsation. It draws in and presses out always and again, like a pump whose handle one moves. Life is not continuous but intermittent. It's not only that it can stop one day; it can always stop.

In a sense, life always recalls itself to life. It resumes, restarts each time and every time that it is not interrupted for too long. Every time that the blood begins again to flow, ejected by the heart and returning to it. It goes without saying [*Il va de soi*] that its composition changes: it deposits certain substances, and takes on new resources. But this is always the blood that flows—*sanguis*, which Latin distinguishes from blood that spills, that flows out and coagulates: *cruor*.

Blood that flows does not cease to flow. Its flow is renewed by the pulsation of the heart. If this pulsation ceases, everything stops. It is in truth a kind of drive: the heart is driven to beat,[3] to contract and to dilate the cavities that compose it. It includes a group of cells (the sinus node) which rhythmically triggers the alternation of the heartbeat. There, in this node, life pushes itself to live. Or is driven to it. It amounts to the same: life receives its own push or undergoes its own drive.

2. Rhythm

Such is life: it receives and gives itself, it is received and given. It comes from elsewhere, since the electrochemical properties of pulsation can be analyzed according to different registers of the non-living. Thus it has been possible, for example, to determine the protein responsible for the regularity of rhythm. Rhythm is equipped with its metronome. Life gives itself that which makes it live. It gives itself life. Just as it takes it away when it stops.

Of course there are other rhythms outside of living beings. Cosmic rhythms, for example. Perhaps we should take seriously the analogy between the universe and the living being. In any case, certain correspondences are manifest: we know that organisms follow the succession of day and night. But the living being manifests rhythm as a drive of its own. The rhythm of the living being exposes rhythm in general as a relation to self. The universe is not a living being, but it expresses in living beings the very fact that it is, that it both makes itself and exceeds itself in the same *coup*, in a single blow: being is more than being, living is more than living. This is a blow that precedes any big bang, the blow of a sudden arrival, of an abrupt flow.

Rhythm is a putting into form. It gives form to what flows. It is not continuous and monotonous, it follows a cadence, it is pulsed: the light beating of an artery beneath the skin is called the "pulse," which in French is the same word as *pulsion* (drive), or pulsation. It can take on various speeds or pacing, according to effort or rest, fever, worry, emotion. It can be subject to a syncope or a spasm. Everything happens as if the body was signaling to itself its pace and even simply its presence.

One can speak of "auto-affection." One can also say that the living being feels itself living and knows itself to be alive. That it is precisely of this that life consists. It feels it and knows it: this feeling-knowing makes up the sense of life. It has no other. It experiences itself as flowing in itself. Flowing away spasmodically pushed and driven toward itself, always exposed to beginning again, or to stopping.

There is also a rhythm that configures fecundity: for the living human being and some other species, the menstrual flow signals the available possibility that another life, that the same life can begin again otherwise. It is a different blood that flows, mixed with other fluids and with what this time was not fecundated. This blood is neither *sanguis* nor *cruor*: it bears the name of its periodicity, *menstruum*. It is another drive and pulsation by which life neither lives nor dies but is moved and shudders from the power to give life. In alchemy, the *menstruum* was reputed to have dissolving properties. The most complex living being retains and also withdraws the life that it propagates.

There is the blood that nourishes life, the blood that leaves it, and the blood that gives it or retains and holds it back. It is the same blood passing through the three moments of living. It is itself the rhythm of living, its live, vital, and lived palpitation—or in the reverse sense: the palpitating push of life rushes on and flows away, both creating and irrigating the living "self," life as "self," both pressed forward and held back from itself. Advance and retreat—without which there would be no self: self approaches itself and separates from self, that is its definition or its essence. In it this back-and-forth or this come-and-go, this alternation and alteration take place like the circulation of blood or the flow of sap.

3. Self (*Soi*)

Self is not defined as a relation to self. Nor as a being "in" itself," "to" itself, or "for" itself. Self is foreign and prior to all these categories. It is foreign and prior to the doubling that these categories assume.[4] No preposition can bind self to itself, since it is not external to itself: *it has always already preceded itself as other insofar as it is itself.* That is why it is blood: fluid under pressure in a closed circuit that nonetheless communicates with all the many outsides of air, nourishment, and elimination. Never does it itself pass outside, or else it ceases to flow and it coagulates. It-"self" as a "same," it is no doubt never this; it is nothing but its circulation, and its communications with the outside occur at its limit (in the pulmonary alveoli or in the intestinal mucosa).

Nor does it ever pass inside: the substances that it transports and distributes leave it just as they have come to it, without diverting the pulsive continuity of its flow. What is true of blood is also true of the other fluids or flows that circulate through the body. It is their general regulator, it gives the rhythm.

Ultimately there is no "outside" and "inside" except in relation to blood: its flow forms the loop of the individual's autonomy. The individual *is* this flow, this flux resembling Heraclitus's river but into which one does not step: it is what moves over and through us and draws us along. On the outside, blood hardens and the living being dies.

But "autonomy" is not a correct term either. What is, is not "by itself" since no preposition is admissible. There is nothing with respect to which it is pre-posed (or in charge [*préposé*]), post-posed, or postponed. Broken down in Greek into *au* and *ton* (in one etymological hypothesis), it can be understood as: "it once more" or "that again." It is the one that returns, which does not mean that it returns to itself. But it makes a return. It is still it, it again and still. Or him, or her. Or X.

Self contains the rhythmic pattern. Which, here again, can be said in the reverse sense: rhythm envelops a *self*. Without rhythm, indeed, *it* can only pass away. Rhythmic, it makes a return. *Self* repeats, that is, recognizes and identifies itself. To identify itself, or oneself, means always "coming to" or "returning to oneself," as we say of someone who has fainted. But it is not a return to the identical: on the contrary, it's a return that had not taken place. Each contraction of the heart is (yet) another. The beat of the heart, the drive of the blood identifies. At the same time, identity finds its scansion.

It is clear that this scansion comes from elsewhere, from a rhythmic knock more ancient or more profound than this beating heart: from a relation already, the one we call "sexual." This relation itself emanates from a more ancient ungraspable beat: from what we name with this poor verb "to be." If something "is," this thing implicates the scansion of space-time, itself doubled into here/there and before/after (each couple demanding the other)—a doubling without which the thing would not exist. A doubling immanent to the "there is."

The archi-originary scansion becomes fully *self* (assuming there is any sense in speaking of fullness or plenitude: there is no complete or finished self, except a dead one) only when it becomes that of an inside/outside: exposed to the air by a breath (in/ex-piration) with which alone begins the regime proper of circulation.

(*Cut! cord, umbilical, jutting-out of withdrawal, syncope, rhythmic mark*)

This more ancient knock is that of repetition: not only one time but several times, once more. It is thus that "there is." There is a beat, and *it* says: "Again!" Why is this?

It assumes that there is doubt, uncertainty: him, is it really him? which him? from where? him, her, *it*? It's a question of provenance, or more exactly it is what arrives with a stranger/foreigner. From where? "Self" is what arrives, what happens, when there is some kind of stranger/foreigner. In this sense, "self" is the complete opposite of the "to itself" or "in itself": it is not a given properness, it is given as improper, as foreign. And foreign in particular to a certain ordering of animal, vegetable, and mineral. Like a virus between living and non-living: it's a parasite, which is to say one that is fed from an other. But then who isn't fed from an other? Is there not a general parasitism? Originally, the *parasitos* was the one admitted to the table of the feast offered to the gods. He is invited by the priests to share the sacred meal, that is, the product of the sacrifice. This assistant is designated by virtue of a function to be carried out, a role to be filled. To him one says: "You, take a place at the table."

But there must first be a meal, and places for those who take part in it. The litters of puppies or piglets lined up along their mother's teats indicate this double possibility: there is food for all and a place for each.[5] Well before the sacred meal and its reversal into parasitism, the possibility of language is given by an originary parasitism. "You, come here!" "Come nourish yourself from the same substance, the one you first found in your mother."

Already there: language says "it's me" or "I'm here" or "here I am" even before speaking, that is, by eating (one does not speak with one's mouth full . . . though one may try to). Which immediately implies the mother's address: "I'm telling you, you who hear it." But then comes the question: "Do you hear me?" "What and whom have you heard?" The interlocutory beat doubles—or exposes—the beating of the pulse. Language is straightaway driven and palpitating. In this sense, it is not added on to an animal organization, it models rather a special animal (in every sense of the word *special*). The self signals (like every living unity), but it relates and reports this signal to itself: it signifies itself. Not as a concept but as the fact that it can designate itself as the same. It signifies itself in the sense that this verb can mean: to make known a decision, a will or intention ("He signaled to him his dismissal"). Self makes itself known as the same—therefore other than you. The other same or the same other. This tension is originary.

4. You (*Toi*)

You: you are not another Self. You are an other than Me, other therefore than Self in a circuit of return. You do not make a return, or at least I cannot undergo your return as mine. And yet you signify to me that you signify yourself, as I do for my part. You are completely other by being completely same. You signify the return of blood not "in you" but "as you." You signify pulsation as repetition of a same that marks off this repetition, which beats its measure or bears this measure before itself as its own.

You: you expose the alterity that is indissociable from Self. You do not return to the same but you return (as) an other same. You return without a doubt and even very certainly from the same, as the same but otherwise, from elsewhere, from another time. Your pulsation corresponds to the same dissociated drive. The dissociation is very old, immemorial. It is contemporaneous with the drive. *It* pulses, therefore it parts—spreads apart and separates.[6] Many forms of life, each time a form that alters, that varies or transforms and that, with language, signifies itself as its own alteration, and, to signal this, says "you."

That is what a form is: the gesture of a distinction that parts and spreads apart, and in doing so distinguishes the other form.

The other form is the beat of your blood which makes a return as yours, just as mine does. And that designates itself as such through this other and similar beat that pushes and presses from me the word "you" which reverberates in yours. Thus we attest to coming altered from the same, from the same as altered, from what comes from nowhere if not from the pulsation itself begun without any beginning, before any before, a push differing/deferring itself, form itself separating itself.

It is this pulsation, which flows like sap and like blood, it is this that is exposed as speech and as this *look* and this gesture in which speech unfolds and in its turn gives a push. You: you are the push that responds and corresponds to itself, and that begins again. You come from this push, like me. It is not anywhere or in any time that lies behind us. It has always-already been divided into places and into moments of origin. It is itself without origin: it is given with the irruption of the universe which does not surge forth in the midst of something else but which only pushes and grows of itself and out of nothing—which is not distinguished from outside itself.

Not in the midst of something else because there is nothing else: but as the midst or medium, the midway of all ways. Each instance of *self* [*chaque coup de soi*], whatever *it* may be, is an unprecedented taking-place. *It happens, it arrives.* In this point, physics and metaphysics merge: impulse and alterity, each one conditions the other.

Self has thus always-already preceded itself without precedent. It has anticipated itself without the least potentiality or possibility. Everything happens in a kind of overflow of nothing or in a superabundance of non-being that makes up the sole substance of what we have endeavored to call "being." This verb that Hegel describes as a "copula deprived of spirit" indicates indeed a relation, one that remains entirely indeterminate. It is not an attribution if it occurs well before any distinction between subject and attribute (quality, property). Nor is it a participation since what comes back does not participate in what came and left: it is an other, the other of the same.

A tautology—"a thing is a thing"—says not that *to auton* is the same [*pareil*] or identical but that it *resembles itself*. And it is thus that the thing at once distinguishes and assembles itself, separates (from), accords (with), and conflicts with itself.

Between you and me, as between self and self, there is neither attribution nor participation. There is repetition of pulsation. Your heart beats and your blood circulates just as do my heart and my *blood*. Just as, or just like: in French *à l'instar de* . . . is an old and studied expression for saying "in resemblance" or "in imitation of." It is said to have first signified in Latin "to be or come in the place of." Resemblance amounts to substitution—or the reverse. Self comes after self and replaces it. It resembles it. And yet it is as impossible to confuse them as it is to confuse me from thirty years ago with me today. Or you with me . . . which are words, echoes of "self"—of *that*, of *it*—repeating and referring to itself as self-same other: coming out of itself to make itself. Coming out of that, of *it*, to do this or that, this and that, this because of that, according to accord and conflict.

For Augustine, the divine world is the world of resemblance, the terrestrial world is that of dissemblance. The second implies the first, of which it is the corruption. The first is essentially the resemblance of man to God. Who resembles no other. Man must resemble the unresemblant, which means therefore that as soon as he resembles anything at all, he dissembles. His model is at an infinite remove, *ad infinitum*, or else it is the infinite.[7]

As soon as we resemble ourselves/each other, we dissemble, you just like me turned toward what resembles nothing. The expression "it's like nothing else" means that a work or the product of a labor conforms to no accepted principles or codes.[8] In fact, no self corresponds to a norm. It consists only in distinguishing itself, in being distinguished, from the indistinct (from *it*). Each distinction is different and each difference defers and differs from the others, *à leur instar, just as* they do.

5. *Instance*

But *instare* is also to push, to insist, to persist, to track and follow traces. From there comes the word *instance*, whose primary sense in French is a pressing demand (from which various juridical and administrative meanings have derived).[9] Self pushes and presses [*soi se pousse*] to its repetition.

Without this repetition it can only disappear. Pulsation is the only means for *it* to arrive—whatever it is, return of the same or coming of the other. In any case, it falls short of or goes beyond these distinctions: *it* takes place only if *it* repeats, since one time—only once—is no time.

The "time [*fois*]" of the once, the event, the blow, the act, the deed, the case, the affair, and even the thing—*it* takes place, it arrives and happens, it comes about and is produced only inasmuch as it is not dissolved in the instant. What is instantaneous in the material, physical sense of the word involves some duration—as for example that of a photographic shutter when one takes what in French is called an *instantané*, a snapshot. If it is only 1/1000 of a second, or even less, duration remains [*la durée dure*]. It is this ineliminable duration that led Derrida to assert that the relation to self differs and defers identity. If we think about it, he thus did nothing other than give to time a role that is no longer only that of the form of internal sense (like Kant), nor that of the negativity of the division of self (like Hegel), nor that of the presence to self (like Husserl, with whom precisely and *at the same time*—as we might well say—Derrida gathers the momentum of his earliest work). Nor does he retain the "temporal ecstasy" of Heidegger, for he discerns in it something of a succession—of the "each time." Time [*le temps*] enjoys an absolute anteriority. *It* will have always-already begun, it will not have done with finishing. Time is just this: that *it* takes place.

In all the roles just evoked, time has essentially the nature or the form of a point, mobile (along a straight line) or multiple (a succession along the same straight line). With *différance*, it is in itself separated of and from itself. One can say that it becomes space-time.

What is important here need not be related to Einstein, even if there are no doubt reasons to do so. What is important is that time is enlarged. It is an amplitude as much as a procession. It takes on at once a volume and a course, indissociably. In fact, it is a body, that is to say, an expansion—as one says today that the universe is expanding. All bodies are expanding or contracting, according to many quite variable modalities. This also means that they all exert a push, a press, if only one that pushes other bodies or else brings them together to form yet others.

The instant has disappeared—or rather it never took place, no more than the point. With time and the body, it is a matter of *instance*: *the body is a pressing demand*, an insistence in its expansion. All the attractions and repulsions, the shocks, the rebounds, or the bondings, are the innumerable encounters of insisting instances, their combinations, their turbulences, and their melees.

Every push has at least a rhythm; each one has its mode of pulsing drive. In one sense, a body is not distinguished from this drive or from the pulsive complexity that is proper to it. It beats in such a way and according to such an arrangement of rhythms and of beats. Bodies are *physical or chemical, living, speaking, cosmic, microscopic, fantasmatic*, even, or *oneiric*: they are always vibrating, palpitating, oscillating, coming-and-going, rhythmed, repeated, diastole and systole—and this is how we come back to blood again.

Blood forms the curvature of space in the coming of time: a body forms, repeats. A body is formed, it is repeated. It grows larger, matures, ages. It insists, persists, perseveres, decays. A body is a pulsive, driven *instance*. Not a single push but an eruption, an emission, an exuberance, and an impetuosity of pressing pushes grasped in a distinct flow and overflow.

Just as in the French language, the pressing instance is transformed into an "authority that decides" and then into a "constitutive factor," likewise pulsation becomes *pulsion*, drive, which in turn begins to resemble an autonomous entity endowed with an authority of its own. Very early on Freud chose the word *Instanz* to designate the unconscious in its distinction and its opposition to consciousness, itself another *Instanz*—a term that, however, he feels the need to clarify by giving as its equivalent the word *System*, which indicates the dynamic complexity that the word *Instanz* might mask.[10] It is above all a question of *insistance*, of an insistent pressure whose entity remains itself unlocatable, itself mobile and fleeting, according to what Lacoue-Labarthe calls a *desistance*—the abandonment to "a breath from elsewhere."[11] *It* has always-already begun. The pressing demand comes from elsewhere—and that is why Freud, when he wants to identify its agent as a drive (*Trieb*), will declare that the drive is a myth. We'll return to this.

6. Glorious Body

Corpus gloriosum magis illuminaret
mundum quam sol.[12]

Such is the other aspect of *corpus*: that which is my body not because it would be my property (or my expropriation) but much rather because *ego sum*, because I am what is formed by the flowing overflow. I am what is pushed in this push; I am insofar as I am pulsed in this distinct manner. If there is something of the "proper" in this, it precedes me and I depend on it much more than it belongs to me.

In its first aspect, *corpus* is divided: bread and wine.[13] In its second aspect, it reunites what is separated, in the absorption of consumption. Bread and wine are distinct, as the dense and the fluid are, also as the grains that compose them are, like the regions and registers of the world with their multiple properties. Absorbed into blood they make up a propulsive flow. Their diversity becomes rhythmic, and the spasms of the heart animate all the contractions and releases, the balances, the oscillations and vibrations of all the organs and tissues. Thus the absorption, this melee in the blood, is not an assumption into unity, it is a redistribution of the manifold. Here *it* oozes and there *it* syncopates, here it draws open and there it squeezes tight. Here it heats up and there it effects an exchange.

In one or another of its aspects, *corpus* does what it does within a complex plural unity. As suggested by the possible provenances of its name, it is form and it is gut: belly or womb. It is distinction—face, for example—and it is confusion—digestion, for example. It is metabolic: in perpetual change, transformation, transition, mutation, or even molting, sloughing off, spasm, emotion.

In all these manners and matters, as they mingle, alternate, and combine, *corpus* passes on and percussively transmits the push from which it arises. This push is one of which it does not and will not ever have any memory—this pulsing drive that preceded all memory and is inscribed nowhere, was itself a melee. Was itself multiple in its unicity. It was a push and a pull, a traction. Or it would have been if it was not already in the process of beating, since always and everywhere, in the immemorial swell of space-time.

Pessoa writes:

> The waves from before all sensation
> Push me, agitate me, occupy
> Torrentially and ardently
> The painful void of my being.[14]

It is this that makes the body: this more-than-primal undertow, primitivity itself as unlocatable, immemorial, and unforgettable, returning from body to body, and in each body from age to age, and within each age from sense to sense, from touch to touch singular plural from every edge, the fringes, margins, and thresholds of a cramped, fragile, and fleeting body.

Thus the body-form is the expansion, the exposure, the skin that offers an outside to the outside. This "here I am" and this "there you are" of skins turned toward one another by their respective contours. Bodies essentially respective and reciprocal. Presenting each other, observing each other, approaching and distancing themselves and each other. Considering and greeting each other,[15] bodies respectful of their mutual boundaries and surrounds—and pushed to approach and edge toward one another when it comes to sex and blood. (Of which we will speak again.)

The hollow: the belly, the gut, the incorporation and assimilation of the outside, and the ejection of waste. The entire world as food and shit. Werner Hamacher writes, in response to Derrida: "'Remains to be known—what makes one shit?' *Glas* will say. Self, or another? Or self *as* other?"[16] This remark hits home [*touche juste*]: as an other to self, Self pushes itself to the point of waste, drives itself to waste. Or it is as the same that it makes itself shit. Can't stand itself. Gets sick of itself.[17] Pushes itself, then, and clears out to make room for the return of the same, or of the other, it's hard to say.

The glorious body is the body ranged along this entire amplitude.

7. Matrix

Now the belly is also the womb [*la matrice*], another push of the other, toward the other as self. Another self detaches. Another other. Otherwise other.

The amplitude of the body is never more ample than with the belly of a pregnant woman—far more than the erect member that penetrated this womb. One and the other, one in the other, these *selves* very carefully divided in two so as to compose another. An altogether other that will be a body of its own, a body apart.

Nowhere does the glory of the body burst out more than in the tense swelling from which another body is born, and in this other new and unknown body, already there but still to come. Everything ready to become "self"—pushing (growing) and pushing away the other "selves."

Every body is the form of a precise beating of the drive. Each time it is the newborn whose form consists of the full and the open, protrusion and hollow, life and death, insistence and desistance, here and elsewhere, it-*self* as *same* unforeseeable to itself and to all. Newborn but always to be born anew, always to become self until it comes to an end one day.

Becoming self *as* the other or the other as self, who can say? This is undecidable because self *is* always *as* an other since it is *to* (it)self: this is inscribed in the oblique case "self." There is no subject case. What *self* wants is to *work its way beyond itself*, as Zarathustra says.[18] In this sense it is, like life, always bound to overcome itself, but the Self is pushed to do, to accomplish beyond . . . And it does this, as Zarathustra also says, *in its eternal return of the same*. It is a work of death that would also be another life, more than life, perhaps death incorporated and reformed, transformed.

A *glorious body*: such is the sense of the body, not only its form transformed into a subtle reality, whose brilliance blinds the dead no less than the living who gather around them—but even more: *transformation itself as form.*[19]

Erect bodies and swollen bodies are transformation as form. They are the form—itself plural—of glorious expansion. Thus glory is indissociably that of all transformations—of lineage, of transmission, of the incessantly other—and that of each singular scansion, of each *self* through which the immense living (or even cosmic) arborescence is related likewise to itself as to something of an other.

And this is not anything other than the Self beyond itself. The Self, always other, coming after itself *just like*—or in the guise of (*à l'instar de. . . .*)—its own insistence. The Self swallowing itself and spitting itself back up, thus at the utmost point of its push and its palpitation.

The glory of the body is the brilliant emergence of an instance borne away into the irradiation of its disappearance. It is a *jouissance* and a failure, a breakdown, the syncope in which the beating that gives it its rhythm is aggravated and ruptured. It is this body itself throughout its existence as a beating movement, insistent alteration and substitution of a self.

Otherwise how do you think there would be this multitude of bodies, of features and contours, of folds, of steps and paces, of speeds and pulsations? All this—all of *it* and every *it*—that swarms of itself? How do you think they encounter each other, mingle, collide, embrace, make themselves known to one another, and even kill one another?

How do you think there would be this abundance, this profusion of lives and of the living? If not from a *matrix*, that is to say from what is neither same nor other but the possibility of transformation by which a form begins to emerge and then comes away, distinguishes itself. It is the origin insofar as it is neither a principle nor a cause but an expansion that began well before, that has always already begun and of which a singular womb [*matrice*], penetrated by another singularity, is but a particular scansion, the beating proper of a self/other.

But there is no womb of wombs, no originary mold. Inasmuch as there is space and time, *it* deforms and transforms itself. It is thus that it is *otherwise other*: *it* is not the other of a "same."

However, it is there that every sort of other (of the) same is formed and transformed. And it is the question of this originary (in)formation that we must pose here.

8. It/Self

(erudite interlude)

It is indispensable to insert here a somewhat erudite *excursus*, so as to justify a usage of the "Self" that may already seem rather bold to some readers. It is evident that the Self [*le Soi*] at issue here is distinguished very clearly from the Ego [*le Moi*], even if it is also the latter's deep and generative layer. In the terms of Freud's second topic, it corresponds to the Id. This might seem surprising, and yet several indications make it necessary to imagine a complex and obscure genealogy of the Id on the basis of the Self.

We know that Nietzsche calls Self (*Selbst*) an *instance* which, he declares, "dominates the ego."[20] Several of Freud's commentators have brought out the analogy. They have done so quite often in order to explain the reference that Freud makes to Nietzsche in terms not of the Self but of the Id. Indeed, when Freud explains the origin of this latter term,[21] he says that he owes it to Groddeck, but he adds immediately—without any other specification—that the latter only follows a usage found in Nietzsche. But Nietzsche's commentators (all of them so far, to my knowledge) have been unable to find in his text the usage in question.[22] However, some of them remark that, all things considered, it is rather the *Selbst* (Self) in Nietzsche that most resembles the Id. Which indeed is incontestable.

The philological question of the origin of the term is thus fairly obscure. This may not seem very surprising. The id—which I will henceforth write without a capital so as not to hypostasize it—does not easily give itself over, even to Freud. The philosophical question of this origin opens onto the most profound enigma—the very one that constantly occupied Freud: the intrication of the speaking being in the mute world from which it arises.

In this respect, the analogy with the Nietzschean *self* is undeniable. It is worth citing the following passage (from the same section of *Zarathustra*):

> Senses and the spirit are only instruments and toys: behind them still lies the self. [. . .] It reigns, and dominates the ego too. [. . .] It inhabits your body, it is your body. There is more reason in your body than in your best wisdom. [. . .] What created respect and contempt and value and will? The creative self created, for itself, respect and contempt, joy and pain.

It would be necessary to comment on these sentences, along with those that accompany them, and in some respects that is what the following pages will do. For the moment, I will simply note that when one reads in German this speech of Zarathustra, keeping in mind the enigma of the provenance of the *it*, one is struck by the repetition of the pronoun *es* which refers to the neuter *das Selbst* (the self). Used as an absolute, *es* can become *das Es* (the it, the id). There is nothing precise to be drawn from this miniscule situation, but one cannot help thinking that a more or less conscious slippage led Groddeck and/or Freud, in reading this page of Nietzsche, to slide from the *self*, with its slightly awkward reflexive air, toward the *it* that designates it while also effacing this reflexivity.[23]

Another passage of Nietzsche[24] provides another possibility—which Freud knew, as did Groddeck—against the illusion of the "I think," which assumes a subject as the master of its thinking, whereas this thinking "comes as it wishes." One must therefore say: It thinks/*Es denkt* (often translated as "Something thinks"). Nietzsche adds, however, that even this "it" is superfluous, for it remains exterior to the thinking process. He does not specify how to do without what he calls a residue of "the evaporation of the good old ego." I will not search any further in Nietzsche for this subject, but it must be noted that if the "it" comes from this passage, it envelops with "thought" a certain reflexivity.[25]

Now as we will see later, it will be necessary to speak precisely of a certain reflexivity.

For the moment, let us introduce here another remark whose erudition is situated on a different level, but not without some relation to the preceding. It has to do with Schopenhauer, in whom Freud recognized very explicitly a precursor of the thought of the unconscious.

As we know, Schopenhauer was also the one whom Nietzsche called his "first and only educator." In the lines quoted a moment ago one finds the word "will"—a central term for Schopenhauer. Now in Schopenhauer, the will is itself only the human name of a deeper and more hidden reality that he calls, after Kant, *the thing in itself* [la chose en soi]. Several remarkable features invite us to relate this thing in itself (as Freud did) to the id/it— and so to think *the thing in id-self* [la chose en ça].[26]

Let us mention only three of these features: on the one hand, as will, it is "essence in itself of our own body, as this thing that our body is besides being an object of intuition and representation."[27] In other words, our body as life and action is that in which the will "expresses itself." On the other hand, this same will does not obey the principle of reason and therefore does not provide a ground to actions of the body. Finally, "in the consciousness that the body has of itself, the will is known immediately and in itself"[28]—and this immediacy implies a reflexivity quite different from that of a consciousness in the full sense of the term.

We can discern how the "thing in itself" according to Schopenhauer can have a certain kinship with the Freudian id (or even with the Freudian topic as a whole). But without going any further in this genealogy, we can add the following: Schopenhauer attributes to this thing a *Trieb*, a drive,[29] and one could thus say that the expression "thing in itself" takes on a singular shape in which it becomes animated. Its "in itself" is not at all an entity suspended in a hinter-world, it is a push, a pulsive drive, whose dynamic mobilizes the world and being-in-the-world.

The idea that the Freudian id takes up where the Kantian thing-in-itself leaves off appears comical at first, but it may well reveal itself to be much more serious.[30]

9. Extension

The culture that was once Western but is now global is a culture of the cause. Or, if one prefers, of "sufficient reason," to use Leibniz's expression. The cause or the reason of a thing is not the thing itself. It is another thing or it is found in another thing. The passage from cause to effect requires an operation that crosses this gap. To be cause of oneself is necessarily the privilege of something that is not related to anything else.

Hence the old idea of God. But in order for God himself not to have a cause, he must not be a distinct being. He must be confounded with the existence of what exists. He is then no longer God: he is that this exists [*que ça existe*].

That it exists: this *it* is not a cause and it has no cause. One could say that it *expresses itself*. But one must still not understand by this an "inside" that would come "out." To avoid this misunderstanding, we may use the more modest word *extension*. What is extended does not pass from inside to outside but is amplified, spread out, distended, disposed, or even dislocated: it is to itself its own matter and form, according to a plasticity, an elasticity, or a ductility that makes up its very being.

Insofar as it is extended, it corresponds neither to an operation nor to a production, no more than to a generation or a growth: these modalities are posterior and secondary with respect to extension. One does not pass from one thing to another, for one is precisely there where things are in the process of distinguishing themselves. Extension spreads apart of and from itself, it is its spreading and spacing apart [*écartement*]—to which corresponds an intensification (or an "in-tension") and therefore a plurality of tensions. Extension is amplification in every sense of the term: spatial volume, vibration, resonance. The best that can be said of it was said by Pessoa:

> The old lyre of that which exists
> Produces sounds that send a shiver.³¹

It is a lyre, or it has one: its sonorities are those of its extension, as the sonorities of a lyre are those of a plucked string, or as those of the flute are produced by the tensed and modulated expansion of a column of air. It resonates, and precisely thus is it-*self*: in itself vibrating and unfolding the reverberations through which it succeeds itself indefinitely. These reverberations send a shiver in two senses: on the one hand they communicate their vibrations, palpitations, and impulses; on the other hand they worry, they anguish, even, for their resonance attests that *it* comes from nowhere, that it is coextensive with a spreading and spacing apart behind which there is nothing.

It has already begun without ever having had a beginning, since everything begins with it. But as soon as it begins, it is extended, it is corporal, and it resonates. *It* is the self of the thing in itself: the push and press of existing.

That indeed is why "without cease, therefore, since the beginning, it is necessary to restretch the skin where the noise of the origin comes to knock."³²

10. Self/Same

The self is not the same. *Sich* is not *Selbst*—one forgets this in languages that do not have a word comparable to this derivative of *selb* which means "same." "Oneself [*soi-même*]" is *sich selbst* and to give to *selbst* the value of "self" is in fact abusive. *Selbst* signifies rather "absolutely the same." It is moreover also an adverb that serves as an intensification analogous to the French expression "quand bien même": even so, all the same.³³

But it becomes "oneself" when it enters into compounds: *Selbstliebe* is "love of self," in which "self" is distinguished from other. "Self" thus means "the same as self" distinguished from a "same as other." By contrast, the French *soi-même*, "oneself" or "itself," does not signify "the same as self" but corresponds to an intensification (as in the Latin *egomet*).³⁴

The self (*le soi*) is identity in itself (*en soi*), the same is identity to another. The two distinguish and mingle, separate and combine themselves. The thing in itself as pressing push engages this disjunctive conjunction: the self pushed is the same as the self pushing, which is to say that they differ between themselves as much as the active and the passive. The self affects itself by repeating itself, and this affect is what makes it; it is its being.

The thing in itself is the *Trieb* according to which *it* comes, is always-already in the process of coming. Space-time, matter, life, language are the reprises, the modulations and intensifications of this same beating—of this beating of the *same*.

That is what Freuds understands in the end, when he writes: "Psyche is extended, knows nothing about it."³⁵

Which also means: I know this (I, Freud), I know this non-knowing but for all that I do not know *that* which it does not know. The extension in question, the expanse or stretch, the being stretched and the drive that pushes it, its pulsation—these are not objects of knowledge. They are rather *the non-objects of non-knowledge* according to which *psyche* is properly what it is.

That is to say, precisely *Trieb*, drive, breath, respiration, panting, inhaling, exhaling. Which has no object, which pushes nothing but itself. Psyche does not inflate any sail, or make a wind turbine spin; but it enters into displacements and into variations of gasses and vapors, into winds, storms, and torpors of plants, of insects, then it is incorporated into the irrigation that palpitates through living beings endowed with blood.

Very precisely . . . except that it has nothing precise or exact. Or rather, it is precise beyond any exactness [*justesse*], any rigor, any congruence. The drive repulses its own identity. It is itself by not repeating itself identically, neither in the formation and animation of a body nor from one body to another in the prodigious diversity that knows no indiscernibles.

Never and nowhere does the drive resemble itself but always and everywhere it is indefatigably the same: the same as that of which there is neither form nor concept. "Spatiality," writes Freud in the same posthumous note, "may be the projection of the extension of the psychical apparatus."³⁶ This *Projektion* is not to be understood in the sense of a representation: it is an enlargement that engenders its amplitude, it is the dilation by which a body goes toward other bodies and at the same time separates and spreads out from them. For there is not one and then another, it is a multitude that arises all at once and that drives and pushes on to its own encounter—all with all—while also repulsing the confusion in which it would return to an empty indifference.

Insofar as it differs and detaches, the Self is at once the motor and the effect of the push. As such it is also its blind spot. As return and succession of the Same, it does not cease presenting itself and eclipsing itself. With it the thing-in-itself loses all possibility of being identified as an essence, as a principle or as an origin. Ruined for this, it sinks abysmally [*elle s'abîme*] in itself and arises from this abyss as the eruption of its depth without ground.

This is also what the extension of Psyche signifies: the flows of lava that spread out from the eruption whose push they prolong and whose ardor they propagate.

11. Excitation

And what a frenzy, what a furor, what fervor in this explosion! Its power is such that it separates straightaway from its own flaming forth. The *bang* is not one. It is both less and more, and in a sense it is no more *big* than it is *slight*.[37] It is without beginning, it bursts open without having been one or initial. The eruption extends and divides itself without anything having taken place that would have been "itself [*elle-même*]," its principle or its essence. And because it is without identity just as it is without past or point of origin—in it on the contrary space-time opens—it is not possible to find in it any other property than its dispersion.

That is why everything that springs forth, each thing, must be itself [*soi-même*]: not first through reflection but through repetition. It presents itself and re-presents itself—without which it would disappear. This goes for a particle or for an organism. Each time it is an aspect, the spark of a push that engages the repetition of presence. Each thing thus perseveres in its being which itself is nothing other than this perseverance. That of a mica, a leaf, or a bear.

It is an excitation: the thing calls itself to itself. That is the sense of *ex-citare*; a call to come out, to compear. *It* compears at the same time to itself—as same—and to other things—as another same, another way to be same, rock or droplet, strand of hair or look in the eye.

It excites / excites itself.

Among all things and within them *it* excites and excites itself prodigiously: it disposes, parts and spreads apart, approaches, weighs, sniffs, confides, mistrusts, defies itself [*se confie, se méfie, se défie*]. Excitation puts into play a general *-fiance*, a question of faithfulness and trust: is it compatible? dangerous? suspect? utilizable? Everything is pushed or repulsed by everything else, by every other. One seeks, one flees, one watches out for and watches over, one surprises and is surprised. These are attractions, repulsions, rubbings, graspings, ingestions, digestions, excretions, perceptions, conceptions—the innumerable modes of excitation. Not a construction but a *struction*, an accumulation without order, without capitalization, heedlessly and wholeheartedly, without calculation and without reserve.

This excitation is not an action exerted on a body from the outside: it is the very push and press that opens a body, detaches it thus from an outside, exposes it to encounters, to attractions and rejections, to graspings and relinquishments, to ingesting and being swallowed, to wounding and being bruised, to killing or to being itself. General formality of the formless in unceasing transformation.[38]

This exteriority or this exposition is inherent to *it*, or to the id. It does not contain or support anything: it is through and through its own extension, which has no properness or property other than dividing itself, dividing nothing, for it has always already begun to do this. Its division precedes *it*. It is deeply and originarily *singular-plural*. And it is this in as many places and times—that is, in as many bodies—as there are.

This extension is an excitation: it pushes itself and pushes again, pulses and re-pulses itself. There is nothing to be distinguished here like bodies and souls, matter and spirit. It is one same thing, the singular-plural thing of the same-as-self whose repetition makes a body.[39] Nor is there any distinguishing between mechanical, chemical, electrical relations, on one hand, and on the other, sensations, sensitivities, sentiments, and sense in every possible sense: the plurality of the singular makes sense straightaway. That is to say, makes being-for-the-other.

12. For

What does "for" mean? "For the love of art" means "because of" or "by virtue of" this love of art. We understand that this love is not a purpose: it is what, in each case, pushes us. Neither the purpose nor the intention that we most easily associate with "for" is primary. These are preceded by a specific sense of cause or dependence, which is that of the Latin *pro*. This sense bears with it an antecedence: it is before, in front of, moving forward, that *for which* [pour quoi] I act. What pushes me to act.

That it would become a goal, an aim, is not surprising: this is called a "final cause." And it is the only true cause, or thing [*chose*]: what pushes and therefore motivates, mobilizes, moves, and is moving (emotion), what sets shaking and gets going. There is no majesty here to give to the other: the other simply forms the shaking movement of the same. And this of course because it is the same in its absolute difference (or *différance*).[40]

The same differs (from)/defers itself. Every identity, every individuality, every atomaticity differs and defers itself: it is only as this transport, this transfer or this transference of self to self, throughout which alteration is not distinguished from being. The other is always-already there. It is this that makes "the" *it*: the enormous, the prodigious metamorphic mass on the surface of which flashes signal lights of identity, a firefly, a toad, a weed, a consciousness in constant transfer from self to other self, from other to other-self.

The other or the outside are only two ways to designate this general push that parts bodies, that separates and spreads them apart, spreads the members of each one, disjoins the times of a rhythm, allows or avoids encounters, shocks, embraces, rejections. "For the other" is not an altruistic slogan, it is a primary and polymorphic constitution: "because of," "by virtue of," "in the direction of," "in the place of," "in exchange for," "for the use of" are so many variants—as often compatible as incompossible—of the one single push.

The push is one and single only according to the polysemy of the verb *push*, which can be transitive or not, and which can exert several kinds of transitivity. From "to grow [*croître*]" to "to press," "to pursue," "to spread apart" or "to set aside [*écarter*]," the differe/ances can have every latitude. They are all modulations of the same effort, of the same tension of existing. It is precisely thereby the materiality of spirit and the spirituality of matter since these two concepts are those of resistance and insistence. Their play contains all ontology. Or the thought of bodies.

Or metaphysics—or metapsychology.

13. Myth

The drives are our myths. This sentence from Freud appears to circumscribe metapsychology, to give it its limits in relation to what ought to be a science. However, Freud's entire approach, and the invention of the term "metapsychology," calls for another understanding. After psychology comes the register of a knowledge that is no longer knowledge of an object but knowledge of what knows itself in its actualization, knowledge that is an act and an experience, one that eludes the possibility of discerning any object or subject of knowledge.

The very last note left by Freud, just after the one saying that "psyche is extended," says this: "Mysticism: the obscure self-perception of the realm outside the ego, of the id."[41] *Mysticism* is not a term frequently used by Freud. Most often it is evoked critically or at least from a certain distance. It concerns the inventions or the fantasms of every form of the supernatural. Such connotations might be present here insofar as it would be a question of denouncing an illusion. But this is not really the case. This "obscure perception" is claimed by no religious doctrine. Everything happens in the space laid out by Freud himself. The obscure perception is a fact, at the very least a fact attested by a "mystical" apprehension. This phrase contains a strange, obscure knowledge of this fact, and this fact itself is an obscure knowledge of the id about itself.[42]

It must be noted, however, that in his emphatic praise of Empedocles—whom he recognized as a precursor—Freud salutes a thought that, although it demands objective exactitude, "did not shrink from the obscurities of mysticism" in its cosmological speculation.[43] He also writes, concerning hypnosis and in a context where it is a question of the formation of the "ego" on the basis of the "id": "There is still a great deal in it [hypnosis] which we must recognize as unexplained, as mystical."[44]

It is mystical because it lies outside the conditions required for knowledge of an object. It is mystical insofar as it is a knowledge that is obscure to itself, a knowledge regarding an obscure perception. To be able to write this surprising note—which he surely found disturbing—it is necessary at least that Freud share something of this obscure perception. It is necessary for him to have a sense of it, a presentiment, a groping sensation. The id perceives something of itself (and I, Freud, I know something of *it*, and I confide it to a note). Even though it is not the ego and therefore is not present to itself. But it is also not completely absent.

The id knows or feels itself, as self. It knows or it feels its own extension not as pure exteriority—for in that case every "self" would be abolished—but as a certain approach or coming of presence. Not to itself but of itself or for itself. What pushes it toward itself as self [*soi*], what pushes toward an imminence of "oneself [*soi-même*]." This for-itself that is for-the-other, thanks to which *it* palpitates, it pulses, and it pushes in every direction, in every sense.

And it is here that we can better understand the phrase about myths. What it says, despite Freud and despite his conscious intention (if there is one, and a single one . . .), is in fact that *myths are our drives.*

This is to say that, for the speaking animal, speech takes up and takes over for every kind of push. It does not replace it but it prolongs it, names it, and makes up its story (for example, with the help of Oedipus).

Speech takes up and takes the drive in its charge. If the drive is the polymorphous *for-the-other*, speech makes of it call and injunction, address and invective, love and hate. That is called myth—which means speech pronounced, sent off as a story (and not simply used as information).

Stories recount where one comes from, where one is going, and how our affairs intermingle. We all come out of the same bellies or on the contrary from incomparable organs. Which blood flows in our veins, and of which origin it attests, with which vigors it is charged. The way it knows how to boil and to spurt.

Myths are our drives because they decline and conjugate and compose our relations: how the other passes from the same to the same, how one substitutes for the other and how the other reappears in another place. How there is defiance and envy, how there are fears and hopes, words with double meanings and others that go unheard or misunderstood.

Myths are what a world, a *cosmos*, says of itself; how it itself says itself. Schelling calls this *tautegory*.

Each *self*, each *it*, in order to repeat and affirm itself, must find itself a story: prince of blood or son of leopard, always it is a question of stories of blood. Its purity or its stain, its gleaming black or crimson, its rising or subsiding. But there are other stories, more discreet or more confused, formed at times in an idiom through which each one's sense is murmured, how it feels to be in the world. An accent and a phrasing proper to each—and for which literature is a magnifying glass or a stethoscope.

Myths are not explanations of the world, as was believed by the thought of general explanation. They are pulsive speech—primary speech: call, injunction, address, warning, threat, seduction. What is expressed among numerous living animals and plants—in the form of colors and odors, dancing and singing, ostentatious display and multiplied shouts—is what first becomes speech for the speaking animal. Tautegory of inexplicable existence.

Which means that the *for-the-other* takes on an autonomy: it is there as such. "Who I am" is a story. "Who you are" is another. "We resemble each other" but "What do you want from me?"—these are continually told and retold, and so on and so forth . . . The speech of the speakers speaks from one to the other, that is, already, from these ones to those others [*des uns aux autres*], and makes of each "one" more than one, and of each "self" an other for/by/to itself. That is the drive: the pulsive beating of the for/by/to, of the same/other, of the singular/plural.

For-the-other is told, tells and tells itself, as for-blood. Blood is the very first material of fiction: father, brother, mixed-blood—whereas milk sets flowing another fiction, mother, sister, and children. Both of them get drunk up, that is to say, they move along the paths of speech and make their way all the way back to silence. Speech *is* the blood that circulates between bodies, which touches and pushes and rhythms the beating pulses of the other.

If I say "I," I take the place of each one and anyone, I identify with everyone and I bring all identity back to me—I who at the same time already *is another*. In saying "you," I identify you with all this, with every *it* [*tout ça*], and I hold you at a distance, non-identifiable. The blood of each one beats its rhythm, and speech beats other rhythms among themselves, from one to the other—the ones to the others and the ones for the others.

That is why blood is apart from the body while also being its life. Blood and speech circulate similarly to and in each other. That is why the myth of *corpus meum* is also that of *sanguis meum*. (And it thus repeats, takes up again, gives renewed impulse to a diffuse mythic element in every tradition.) One often forgets this, but that is how the story goes, in two phases: this is my body, this is my blood. Eat and drink. *Sôma* and *aima*, flesh and blood, the body and its animation. Blood is therefore distinct from the body, as the rhythm is distinct from the drum. Blood is as mythical as it is physical. The pulsive drive is bloody, and blood pulses and palpitates.

14. Sacrifice

"To sacrifice" signifies carrying out a sacred act. "Sacred" is what is withdrawn from humans and reserved for the gods. This can be blessed or accursed, consecrated or condemned, or even both together: the domain of the gods contains threat and salvation. The first sacrifice was human sacrifice. It seems that nearly every culture has known it. The substitution of an animal for a human being is only a substitution. Something of the human must be sacrificed: in the West, everything begins with two deaths destined to send humans beyond themselves. One is Socrates, the other is Christ. (Before this there was Iphigenia and Isaac.)

In blood sacrifice, blood flows out of the body. *Sanguis* becomes *cruor*. It is another substance, one that is no longer contained in pulsation but rather spurts out. It can be drunk, it can become the blood of another, another blood. It quenches the thirst for the other, which is the thirst for the other life. Not only that of a divine world but the thirst for the life of the other, since the other lives the same life as me and yet lives it for himself.

To take in blood is to take in flesh. *Cruor* comes from a Sanskrit word for "flesh [*chair*]." It gives the Greek *keras* and the Latin *crus*, the broken or wounded leg. The entire immemorial obsession with open, bleeding, blood-soaked flesh . . .

The for-the-other thus manifests that it pushes no less to take the life of the other than to receive it. Sacred ambivalence is in play here: the other self must precede and I must precede it—since after all nothing legitimizes any priority. Everyone succeeds and their succession itself shows them that by right each one precedes infinitely. We are therefore equals *and* rivals for the same reason: *we are all first and second*.

Protohistoric anthropology tells us that sacrifice would be the first form of "distribution-sharing" (*partage*) in community, the obscure origin of law.[45] From here too the sense of the word *sacrifice* comes to be split between the fact of consecrating to the gods and that of renouncing something or someone. Sacrifice is based on the possibility of considering another as myself, or at least as belonging to or having a "share" in myself.

That is why the drive speaks of the origin, names it and calls it. It is a matter of being the origin and consequently also of preceding it or getting behind it. I must get behind—and for that I must exceed myself and become the other. I must therefore also substitute myself for it. In sacrifice,

I spill the blood—the life and the sense—of the other and I recuperate it thus as my blood.

Every murder is on this basis a sacrifice that is unaware of itself because its economy of substitution is lost or repressed. And each domination is a murder unaware of itself in an analogous manner. But always the same desire circulates: the desire to feel palpitating in oneself the blood of the other, to feel pulsing the originary blood.[46]

The desire to live is not the simple desire to persevere: it is the desire to begin absolutely, to re-begin the beginning that never took place. It is a push, the push itself, the drive that is indissolubly nervous, visceral, and linguistic. Or rather pre-linguistic: the resonance of the *id* in itself, this resonance in which it is *self* and repeats itself and seeks itself, immediately lost and lost in sum at the heart of itself.

From that point, and straightaway, it must overcome itself in order to come about, and it must feel the other vibrate with a vibration proper to *self*. Everything is ready for the sacrifice. The spilled blood communicates the excitation of the pulsation that spurts out and exhausts itself in this spasm. The incredible, terrifying, and monstrous *jouissance* of murder is there, gathered densely into itself.

In spurting forth, *cruor* resonates or palpitates like an origin that would surge up there where a life is ruptured. That is why sacrifice is the great fantasm, the ritual of the impossible: *cruor* would become a new *sanguis*, newness itself.

This is crude [*grossier*], it is only mimicry and parody. But at the same time as one discovers this crudeness one also learns the power of dominating, which makes up the murder that is inherent to sacrifice and that perpetuates itself well beyond any rites, to the point of intoxication in a massacre, of an extermination that would produce a regeneration, or, in another version, the selection of a superior blood.

The more humanity has substituted for sacrifices the service to a domination that is itself extended to all things, the more it has appeared to itself as sacrificing no longer chosen victims but crowds, peoples, lineages, and generations, as if the new blood had to be that of an energetic and indefinite process of production and transformation, an origin always to come. Thus cruelty tends to become permanent and polymorphous, making blood flow—symbolic, economic, and psychical blood—and above all losing sight of the very possibility to feel the beating of a new blood.

15. Torture

It would seem that humanity is placing itself under torture [*au supplice*]: that is to say, in the kneeling position of one who supplicates a power able to spare them.[47] This supplicant has thus already suffered and dreads the prolongation or the aggravation of this suffering. Sacrifice concentrates the suffering on the tortured, thus all at once excluded by their spilled blood and reintegrated by the absorption of this blood into the body of the others. Cruelty on the contrary extends without measure a suffering sought for itself.

How is that? The push and press of modern domination has withdrawn all justification of sacrifice even as it has maintained the demand to spill blood. It is no longer for the consumption of priests and the faithful that spilled blood is destined, but for the maintenance of an apparatus that transforms it into energy for production and domination. This apparatus presents itself as a necessity, since by harnessing the life of the greatest number it assures this life that it can live. It is precisely thus that one maintains the victim so as to present it as in fact alive and as consenting to the sacrificial knife. Everyone is henceforth consigned to this existence of outcasts to be maintained in a state of supplication: everyone demands to live, to continue to survive, since there is nothing else to demand. The price paid for this is the shameless enrichment of some people who only make more evident a general dependence on an anonymous and automated domination. For these wealthy people do not present even the slightest semblance of an existence that would be valuable for itself.

The body of the tortured, of the supplicant, is reduced to kneeling. The industrial nineteenth century invented the expression "the damned of the earth": the sufferings of hell are now those of the living beings reduced to maintaining their existence in misery, labor, and the absence of any perspective other than submission to the apparatus.

In the twentieth century, Artaud could write: "Existence itself is a superfluous idea [*une idée de trop*]."[48] He wrote this at the very moment when the philosophies of existence were attempting to think an ecstasy of being. An ecstasy, that is to say an exit of the same from itself. By which it would find itself in losing itself, in its very loss. Not through the dialectical profitability of its expenditure, not through a return on investment, but in the experience of the "too much [*trop*]": I overflow myself, *it* overflows me. "The *ego* is liberated only *outside itself*," as Bataille summarized it.[49]

This *outside* is as ecstatic as it is torturous [*suppliciant*]. For it is unbearable, designed as it is precisely not to be bearable. The death of each one of us has this double character. In other words: ecstasy essentially eludes the one who would want to live it, and torture comes to everyone who goes through what is intolerable in a life exposed to death.

Is this to say that the violence of this exposure must be expressed in the "earthly damnation" of a world made up on the one hand of monstrous suffering (camps, bombs, slums, hunger) and on the other of empty satisfactions (like a tower three thousand feet high, or every form of "big data" imposed on the incalculable)? If we must answer *yes*, then that means that from sacred sacrifice to the tortures of inanity, humans would have run through the entire cycle of their pulsation. It would not be surprising if this pulsation came to an end in a cruelty that it would not even be able to recognize as its own.

Marx writes that "capital comes into the world dripping with blood."[50] This is not mere rhetoric, and it concerns not only the past. The chapter that this sentence concludes brings together earlier texts from which it will suffice to provide one example (Marx is quoting from John Fielden):

> In many of the manufacturing districts, but particularly, [. . .] in [. . .] Lancashire, cruelties the most heart-rending were practised upon the unoffending and friendless creatures who were thus consigned to the charge of master-manufacturers; they were harassed to the brink of death by excess of labour . . . were flogged, fettered and tortured in the most exquisite refinement of cruelty; . . . they were in many cases starved to the bone while flogged to their work and . . . even in some instances . . . were driven to commit suicide . . . The beautiful and romantic valleys of Derbyshire [. . .] became the dismal solitudes of torture, and of many a murder. The profits of manufacturers were enormous; but this only whetted the appetite that it should have satisfied, [. . .] they began the practice of what is termed "night-working," that is, having tired one set of hands, by working them throughout the day, they had another set ready to go on working throughout the night.[51]

It must be remembered that this is where we come from. But today what we've come to are calculated exhaustions, programmed and accompanied moreover by periodic catastrophes and disasters which are themselves programmed. Let us cite only these sentences: "The exploitation of work today is no longer based on the promise of gaining wealth, but on the threat of downward mobility, poverty and misery. Employers give this threat the form of what the appellate court has called 'management through fear.'"[52]

Hope has given way to fear: the fear of being sacrificed, we and those who come after us, by a machine that crushes not only human energy but also familiar points of reference, the marks or traces of a sense of existing. Fear, then, not only of violent death but of a death infused into the veins of a managed life.

Four centuries ago, Pascal already felt the need to write this: "There is an infinite distance between the prohibition God placed on killing and the speculative permission that your authors [certain theologians] have given to do it."

Now this "speculative permission," aggravated not by theologians but by the speculators who have replaced them, still forms a principle inherent to the entire techno-economic order that we have developed. Thanatos has no doubt never given Eros so much competition—unless it has sacrificed the latter to its desire.

16. Embrace

It is not sufficient to become indignant or terrified. We must begin by recognizing the drive, the driving force of all the identifiable drives (if they are identifiable): the surge that beats against the edge of the senseless.

It is the same surge, both similar and other, that beats when bodies embrace. They are on the edge of sacrifice, but in a way that is completely the opposite. It is not about making *sanguis* spurt out as *cruor* but of spreading and spilling into each other by and through the other. There is no torture, but there is a kind of supplication—take, receive, come, again, ah! The embrace brings about the most frantic pulsation, the most primal, the most repetitive, and the most uncouth. Bodies get lost in it, dismembered in fragments of *it* and in incandescences of *self*. Saying "yes" saying nothing proffering a raucous nothing of sense.

This traverses times, ages, genders, even sexes. It is more and less than sex, it is the foam that does not cease to form on the waves of the unlimited. This foam is the other aspect of blood, not the flow but the froth that does not coagulate and that disperses.

They could tear each other apart, these bodies, and lose all their blood in each other. We thus have a notion of the morbid violence in sexual obsession, and in rape which is often also a murder. We understand that there is in this a rage to fulfill and to finish off: the impossibility of letting blood beat and letting all this, letting *it* stir around at random. We understand that the entwining of speaking bodies signifies that they are pushed, each of them, to originate the other in order to originate oneself. Perhaps this is even the sense of the words "I love you"—even more radically than "I desire you." For "I love you" means, at the furthest point of the oblative and at the furthest point of possessiveness (it is the same point): I want to be your origin, what immediately carries away the origin plain and simple, the origin of every other.[53] (It could also be that I want you to be my origin: this changes very little in the tendency toward annihilation of one or the other.)

And why is this? Because language consists in bringing itself to the origin, essentially and in each case. And it is this that we call "*jouissance*" or "joy"—inasmuch as *it* pushes itself (and thus pushes us) toward it, toward *that*.

It is at this point that we must come back to Freud's last note: "Mysticism: the obscure self-perception of the realm outside the ego, of the id."

It is therefore capable of perceiving itself. Which is to say that in an obscure way it possesses the property of consciousness. We could say it thus: the unconscious is conscious of its unconsciousness. Which can also be turned in this way: the unconscious is unconscious of its consciousness. (What we are touching on here is in fact the limit of the use of the words "conscious" and "unconscious." The first implies too much reflexivity, representation, and mastery: conscious states can be more or less devoid of these. The second implies too much simple negativity, a sort of pure absence—whereas one may well and no doubt should imagine that it feels itself [*s'éprouve*] in some way. One would think we were faced with a couple consisting of a high-performance robot on the one hand and on the other a stone; but with this we will never have a speaking animal.)

We can approach this strange "consciousness" on the basis of what emerges from the identity between "it" (or "id") and "self"—between *Es* and *Selbst*. The latter is directly implicated in *Selbstwahrnehmung*, perception of self or auto-perception. *Selbst* is the intensive or superlative form of *Selbe* (same).[54] In perceiving itself, *it* perceives itself in its resemblance to self. By nature an obscure perception . . .

The *same* according to which *it* makes (it)self, each time as a self, a body that does not cease to start again, to remake itself—including in the mode of undoing itself—this *same* perceives itself confusedly as the same-so-the-other, as other-so-the-same. The speaking body is the body that can address—to itself as to the other—this altered sameness. And it is precisely language that alters it: for in saying "I," I substitute you for myself in the unsubstitutable place from which I speak. You tear apart my throat which you open. I am in relation with you through this tearing apart.

Mystical, this perception, since it escapes every experimental or deductive confirmation. Reason can only push it aside, but in doing so, it indicates it and stutters out this "obscure self-perception of the id."[55] This obscurity is one in which the same is not distinguished from the other even as it senses itself as other through its sameness. In which the embrace is not distinguished from the encounter—without, however, ceasing to be distinguished from it—the embrace threatening the encounter with disappearance even in promising to fulfill it, the encounter holding this threat/promise at a distance.⁵⁶

Between me and you this tension is not calmed; it remains both desire and threat, abandonment and domination. The obscurity in which this perception takes place envelops the truth. The German *Selbstwahrnehmung*—self-perception—can be broken down as "grasping (the) true (of the) self" or "true grasp of self."

17. Justice

If law begins in sacrifice, and if this unassignable origin turns out to be a hemorrhage in which speaking life would be exposed to the possibility of cruelty—to say it with Derrida: "the drive [. . .] of evil for evil's sake, of a suffering that would play at enjoying suffering from making-suffer or from making-oneself-suffer *for pleasure*"⁵⁷—the pleasure of assigning oneself to the origin at the price of being annihilated in it with the other—then law itself, that is, every disposition for regulating relations between speaking beings (as well as between them and other beings), must be referred to the truth that exceeds it: the obscure detachment of each self and its no less obscure attachment to all of *it*, to the entire *it* and *id* [*à tout le ça*].

Located at the disjunctive conjunction of the two is the just and precise measure—which is not to be found since it is lost in mystical obscurity. But it is thus that justice can be pronounced: it shows itself here for what it is, namely a word, something spoken, an oath, a declaration. *Ius orare, ius iurare, iusiurandum*: justice must be said, speech is not there for anything else. It is thus that it takes the drive in charge and that, in turn, it pushes and pulses. Thus it is never exclusively juridical speech but always also philosophical, literary, and poetic all the way into the secret heart of every *juris-diction*.

Like blood it pulses, and can spurt out from a violent blow and coagulate. It can make itself cruel. Like blood, it can irrigate itself, pronouncing nothing other than its very beating.

In what conditions, in what way to speak *most precisely* and thereby most *justly*? How to say "and me and you" in such a way that the "and" is exact, that it not slip toward "is" or "have"?⁵⁸ Such exactness [*justesse*] and justice cannot be signified: it is found only in a tension of speech that at times appears as song, at times as silence. A pulsation that doubles the pulse of blood in our arteries.

This pulsation—no juridical or political practice should ignore its anxious restlessness. No civilization and no civility can do without this mystique. Which itself is necessarily also a poetics in the most sober sense: a just word that carefully takes up silence, making it resonate. It is thus that we must read these last notes of Freud: let us not introduce a cleavage between *it* and *me/you*. Let us not claim to justify either of these, neither the violence of the drives nor the autonomy of a "subject." Let us acknowledge that they are indissociable and that justice consists in recognizing this fact while also knowing that this recognition cannot be grounded in reason.

18. Sublime

If it is not a question of adjusting the just in some way that would do without approximations, negotiations, and incessant restarts of restlessness, could we say on the contrary that what has been called the "sublime"—the aesthetic and affective category of a passage to the limit of pleasure—might have a place here?

For such a place must be occupied, however unlocatable or untenable it may be. Perhaps there is no civilization without some kind of sublime, whether it's a question of works or of acts. But this must not be confused with the magnificent or the grandiose. In that respect we must turn away from the word itself, which seems to qualify a state or a being, and turn toward sublimation as the Freudian name for the process by which a drive-bound violence appears to be overcome in a spiritual expression.

I indeed say "appears" for it is precisely this overcoming that is not certain. Freud recognizes that artistic sublimation exceeds the grasp of psychoanalysis. He recognizes this in relation to Leonardo da Vinci, and in a commentary where without any other specification he evokes Spinoza.[59] And what is at issue in Spinoza if not the movement of the effort or the push—*conatus*—through which is exerted the desire of a being to be itself? The force of this push is called *virtus* and this virtue is nothing other than the power of what acts according to its proper nature.

As we know, *The Ethics* declares just before its conclusion that "beatitude is not the reward of virtue but its very exercise." We can translate: enjoyment, *jouissance*, is not a satisfaction but the act, the tension of the act in being as properly *self* as it is possible to be. This act for Spinoza can only be actualized in the love of "God or Nature," that is, in the participation in the proper essence of the infinite, an essence that is bound up with its energy or its desire to be.

If this is indeed what Freud glimpses in the secret of the powerful sublimation in play with da Vinci, then this means that there can be a way to escape from the drive-bound trap of destructive *jouissance*. But it is not a question of some kind of gentle sweetening. Neither in an aesthetic register nor in that of love. It is a question of an *integral transport of force* that pushes on to its liberation, in the sense in which one speaks in physics of the speed that liberates from gravitational attraction. Pulsation liberates itself in a space where it resonates only with itself, that is to say properly with all the others no less than apart from all.

What remains a secret—the secret of what one calls "beautiful" or of what one calls "love"—is held in this absolute beating of the drive.

19. But Still Again

That is not all. There is no "all." No completion or fulfillment. What does not begin does not end. And that is finitude: a fold of id, the same fold that differs/defers its sameness. All signification withdraws from it. Language "indicates the sovereign moment when it can no longer take place" (Bataille). But precisely, and *just so*, it indicates this. It does nothing but that, nothing but *it*: it does nothing but pulse this sovereign moment. Impulse it, expulse it, compulse it and compile it . . .

Thus must we think that a just poetics—not only literary but pragmatic, social as well as artistic, in friendship or in love—is decidedly the only possible counterweight to domination. A politics cannot suffice for this, but must on the contrary reserve beyond itself the space of this poetics.

Freud asked if civilization had not demanded too much mastery over the drives, which would come to claim their due. But today we learn the inverse: civilization channels everything into a drive of domination that suffocates itself. What we need is more "sublime"—or to avoid the trap of this word: more elevation, more *élan*, more lightness, breath, halo or *sfumato*, to recall da Vinci, who perhaps painted in order to enchant the silence.

The drive itself withdraws its signification. The pulse beats no more, the beat becomes eternal.

This moment is one in which bodies distinguish and desire each other, in order to recognize each other and to deny each other, to succeed and to substitute for each other. "Me and you" is the same as well as the absolutely other *for the same reason and in the same relation*. This relation that always relates itself to an infinity never begun, never forgotten, never present or absent, and always sovereignly between us.

> It gave itself into Your hand:
> a You, deathless,
> at which all I came to itself. Wordfree
> voices drove around, forms of void, everything
> entered them, mixed

and unmixed
and mixed
again.⁶⁰

20. Life Is Cruel

That life is cruel—this has been said, written, and sung as much perhaps as "life is beautiful." And in any case we know that the second formula is meant to be comforting, whereas the first is simply true. This truth is modern—not because people's lives in the past weren't hard, unjust, painful, or oppressive but because the cruelty of life has to do with another kind of suffering. We can—at least for the purpose of giving it a point of reference—see it appearing with Baudelaire, both in the actions of staged characters and in the images inflicted on the reader. It will suffice, here, to recall these lines:

> You would have the entire universe passing through your bed,
> Impure woman! Boredom makes your soul cruel.
> To exercise your teeth in this singular game
> You need a new heart in the rack each day.
> Your eyes, lit up like shop windows
> Or like blazing lamp-stands at public festivals,
> Insolently use a borrowed power
> Without ever knowing the law of their beauty.
>
> Blind, deaf machine, fecund in cruelties!
> Salutary instrument, drinker of the world's blood,
> Why are you not ashamed and why have you not seen
> In every looking-glass how your charms are fading?⁶¹

Without entering into a longer analysis, we can note two things: boredom[62] makes this soul cruel and its cruelty is that of a blind and deaf machine. Boredom is a modern evil in that it is produced by an absence of interest, of passion, and of sense. No need to say anything more about the machine—one that is above all blind and deaf, detached from any worker or project.

Baudelaire's contemporary Lautréamont made his Maldoror a being who is essentially cruel—but who only repays in kind the author of the world:

> I saw the Creator, spurring on his useless cruelty, burning fires in which old men and children perished! It is not I who begin the attack: it is he who forces me to turn him, like a top, with the whip made of steel ropes.⁶³

The Creator's cruelty (note the assonance) is useless, and this strips his creation of all value, while in return it evokes what Maldoror elsewhere calls his "genius in cruelty."

Still caught in the trappings of an inherited poetics, this cruelty expresses a misfortune that is no doubt irreparable, but we still know what it is supposed to negate ("are you not ashamed?" . . .). Less than a century later, it becomes, with Artaud, a necessary and vindicated violence:

> Without an element of cruelty at the root of every spectacle, the theater is not possible. In our present state of degeneration it is through the skin that metaphysics must be made to re-enter our minds.[64]

Even less than a century later it becomes necessary to define man by the furthest point of cruelty:

> If man laughs, if he is the only one, in the animal kingdom, to exhibit this atrocious facial deformation, it is also the case that he is the only one, going beyond the egoism of animal nature, to have attained the supreme and infernal stage of *cruelty*.[65]

For Aristotle, laughter, which like language is specific to man, sets off involuntary thinking.[66] For us, it is the mark of a deliberate will to do evil and to cause harm. Must we sum up this ellipsis as the advance of a culture that has thought of itself as the ultimate fulfillment of civilization? Must we consider that what has been accomplished is exactly what philosophies and religions have considered properly inhuman, the voluntary perpetration of murder (whether overtly bloody or the work of hunger, misery, exploitation, and manipulation)?

Must we admit that human life—that is to say life, absolutely, becoming a question for itself—is doomed to destroy itself—and with it to destroy life, absolutely?

21. Eros, Thanatos, Cosmos

In *Civilization and Its Discontents*, the same work in which he inquires into the repression of the drives and its reversal into the drive to destruction, Freud revolves around (so we can describe it) the Christian commandment to love one's neighbor, the latter being "understood both as each one and as all together." He evokes it quite early in his text and sets out to demonstrate that it is a "*Credo quia absurdum*," as he puts it in chapter 5. This religious absurdity represents at the same time for Freud the extreme degree of pressure exerted by the super-ego on the drives.[67] Later, in chapter VIII, Freud speaks of what is "especially interesting" in this commandment, when it is faced with the difficulty of containing the "constitutional inclination of human beings toward aggression" (SE 21, 142). But then he immediately declares it inapplicable and therefore "an example of the unpsychological procedures of the cultural super-ego" (SE 21, 143). At the same time, however, he states that it is "the strongest defense against human aggressiveness" (SE 21, 143).

At that point we are very close to the end of the book, and this end will affirm that what remains, in face of the degree attained by modern violence, is to "hope that [. . .] eternal Eros will make an effort to assert himself in the struggle with his equally immortal adversary." A final sentence adds: "But who can foresee with what success and with what result?" (SE 21, 145).

It is therefore with a fragile hope for an upsurge of Eros that Freud's study concludes—the same study that has set aside the love, so powerful and so absurd, of the Christian commandment. From one love to another . . . the situation does not lack for a certain piquant irony, if we can put it thus. The commandment ought to be substituted by desire, but in a way what is at stake is a displacement or a substitution within the same sphere of "love."

One can note here—as Freud also could have done, all the more in that he insisted on the relatively recent character of the commandment[68]—that Christian love emerged in Rome. Which is to say that this singular invention arose in the context of the first civilizing violence of a modern type. This violence consists in effect of a composite of law and administration, military and urban engineering, and finally domination of a conglomeration that corresponds neither to a people nor to a kingdom but to the management of a mastered diversity. This world is also one overtaken by "a strange sadness," as Freud states elsewhere.[69] The impracticable commandment arises in direct response to the first entrepreneurial sociopolitical practice. Rome is a world in disarray, a world of lost reference points and religious confusion. It is an order that is intolerable to those who are not satisfied with wealth, an order of violence that calls forth the invention of its "most powerful antidote," which will later be placed in the service of domination itself.

That Freud did not explicitly make this connection does not mean that he did not have a keen awareness of the singular character, whether irritating or disconcerting, of the commandment of love. He does not discern perhaps what could simultaneously distinguish and bring closer this love of Eros that he substitutes for it. The long and abundant discussion of the couple "Agape and Eros" had not yet taken on the public dimension it would later assume[70] (which in fact it has always had across all the Christian theologies and spiritualities of love but which has remained the least visible element of the religion in both its Roman and Protestant versions).

For in the end it is indeed a question of "civilization," that is, not what would characterize the West but—since the West can itself only recognize this by way of everything that escapes it (the East, the South, the Archipelagos), which in every circumstance or geotechnical situation allows for a composition of existences, of symbols and drives. That is to say, what one can call a world, or in a more eloquent manner a *cosmos*: a totality that is composed by itself in view of itself. What Freud recognizes in modern violence—and what we are experiencing today—is the possibility of the rupture of such a composition.

Freud himself gives very little attention to the *cosmos* despite several significant occurrences.[71] However, he himself remarks, when he examines the genesis of Judaism and then of Christianity, the importance first of the world of pharaonic domination then of the confusion created by the Roman world in the formation of the double religion. Everything happens as if the question of *Discontent*—of malaise—were that of a world that has become so violent that it destroys it, so violent that in the absence of Christian love an upsurge of Eros became necessary—despite the obscure complicity between the two eternal partners.

Perhaps then, thanks to Freud and moving beyond him, we can understand that Christian love involves something completely different from Eros in that it puts into play a world rather than relations between individuals. Stripped of its religious clothing,[72] *agape* is understood as the possibility of welcome, that is, of what allows for exchange, coexistence, the composition of reasons and of passions. It is an act that opens a space of compossibilities (to speak with Leibniz), which is to say a *cosmos*: no less the compossibility of all things than the form that composes itself from them, a *cosmetics*.[73]

This would mean that Judeo-Christian love constituted from the beginning a demand issuing from the feeling of an acosmism, of a lack of world in the globalizing process [*mondialisation*] that was just getting underway and that would eventually prosper. That is why it makes the demand to accord, to give value to everything that makes up a world. And that is why it is not opposed to Eros and Thanatos and is not in rivalry with the couple they form.

22. Drives without Objects

The greatest misunderstanding or the greatest confusion of our entire civilization surely has to do with the inextricable polysemy of the word "love." This polysemy is not accidental: we have given the same name to desire and to recognition. Desire has objects—of enjoyment and/or of destruction—whereas recognition knows places, signs, values.[74] In the world of the "general equivalent,"[75] two phenomena occur: on the one hand an abolition of recognition, on the other hand a promotion of objects. The two are conjoined or perhaps are a single thing, a general objectalization whose primary manifestation is the production of objects, which includes also the production of those objects that are the agents of production themselves: human beings and all the existent species enrolled in the service of production, which tendentially has approached universal totality.

In this way, universal production, tending toward autoproduction, tends also toward the dissolution of the *cosmos*—if at any rate a cosmos supposes a welcoming disposition of values, that is, above all, not prices fixed by a market system but evaluations that are recognized as such among themselves and that recognize their own and each other's places.

Here we find cruelty again: it consists in nothing other than the reduction of forces of evaluation to objects. These latter are provided first by life, whose ground is the it/self. Let us recall Nietzsche's phrases: "What created respect and contempt and value and will? The creative self created, for itself, respect and contempt, joy and pain."

On the basis of the it/self a world can be created and with it a recognition. Provided that it not be replaced by an equivalence. That is to say, provided that alterity not be vanquished by sameness. Provided that the similar, the *semblable*, recognize itself as the *other* of the similar. But in spilled blood—in *cruor*—there is the possibility of reduction to the same, to the equivalent object, from the moment at least when there is no sacred to guarantee and sanction its sacrifice.

But there is no sacred unless there is a world, a *cosmos* in which places and roles can be recognized, rather than objects distributed.

The drives by themselves are not productive of objects. Freud knew this very well. He writes, in conclusion to his remarks on homosexuality: "We are thus warned to loosen the bond that exists in our thoughts between drive and object. It seems probable that the sexual drive is in the first instance independent of its object; nor is its origin likely to be due to its object's attractions."[76]

A little later in the same text he will stress that "under a great number of conditions and in surprisingly numerous individuals, the nature and importance of the sexual object recedes into the background." To which he later added this note: "The most striking distinction between the erotic life of antiquity and our own no doubt lies in the fact that the ancients laid the stress upon the drive itself, whereas we emphasize its object. The ancients celebrated the drive and were prepared on its account to ennoble even an inferior object;

while we despise the activity of the drive in itself, and find excuses for it only in the merits of the object" (SE 7, 149).

We must be attentive to the vocabulary used here: "celebrate," "ennoble," "excuse"—there is here a stark contrast between two worlds, one of which honors the drive whereas the other respects only the object. In an analogous manner, Freud explains elsewhere: "If we were inclined to suppose that savage and half-savage peoples were guilty of uninhibited and ruthless cruelty towards their enemies, we will then be very interested to learn that in their case too the killing of a man is governed by a series of precepts which are included among the usages of taboo."[77]

The least that one can say is indeed that genocides, atomic or cluster bombs, as well as child prostitution, forced sexual acts, and all work that is no less coerced for being paid, as well as the more or less indirect poisoning of food, air, and water, even the pollution of space (of the late great *cosmos*)—this entire evocation of our actuality attests to an absolute privilege of objects, in service of which the drives are in fact subjugated.

If modern religion or religions have deployed (reversing the sense of their invention) an unheard-of super-egoic cruelty (which Freud never ceases to insist on), it is to the extent that they have been submitted to the acosmic organization of the production-consumption of objects in which enjoyment, or the pulsive joy that is tendentially without object, is lost.

A world, on the contrary—a *cosmos* in which to find (a) place according to life and death, according to the inanimate and the animate, according to dreams and the real—is there where, in Hölderlin's phrase, *alles ist innig*[78]—everything is intimate (and one could add with Augustine: "more intimate than the intimate").

Or else, as Virginia Woolf wrote, it is there that "we are the words, we are the music, we are the thing itself. And I see this when I have a shock."[79] Or Hermann Broch: "Isn't what we hear in music nothing but our disappearance, nothing but the soundwave bouncing and vanishing in the distance of breath emanating from the grass, emanating from the clouds, the echo of existence that arrives and vanishes in the distance?"[80] Or Aurélien Barrau: "But the miracle of living beings is that which is fragile as such. It is what is intrinsically precious. The beautiful that precedes art."[81]

There would be so many other texts . . . , or else images, like a photograph by Valérie Jouve;[82] or songs such as "Valse hesitation"[83] by Rodolphe Burger, and so many other mythical—or mystical—constructions of a cosmos within which alone it is possible to live, to die, to pulse, a mythical cosmos, that is to say speaking of itself—tautegorical—so that all its myths can speak there, for example, Eros, Thanatos, Polis, Civitas, Agape, Islam, Scientia, Ruah, Kallos . . .

Valérie Jouve, *Untitled (Characters with Josette)*, 1991–95. C-print, 100 × 130 cm. Courtesy galerie Xippas, Paris, and Valérie Jouve.

In place of the same's knocking against its sameness, the it/self takes in everything and perceives it in its "obscure self-perception." It makes it beat with the living beat of the drive—that of "life death."[84]

That is why it is for us less a question of protesting against cruelty and of a program for overcoming it than of extinguishing it here, now, in the present—not through a regression—illusory—of our (false) world but through "a further increase of civilization, of freedom, or even of a reason sublimated and driven beyond its habitual limits."[85]

Sublimated, yes, in the sense I indicated above, that of an integral transport of the force of a drive toward an object that is a form yet to be born and not an object to produce. Which can take place only in the vicinity of a *cosmos* and through a *poietic* work—such as the one that Michel Deguy designates thus: "Let us repatriate into man the divine oxymorons"[86]—by which we can and must understand above all the oxymoron of Eros and Thanatos.

Right away, it's urgent. Perhaps there is in fact no more time and a cruel destiny awaits its fulfillment. Perhaps.

—*Translated by Jeff Fort*

Longing for the Father

1

Vatersehnsucht: This is how Freud designates the first relationship—primal, archaic in the most literal sense—indispensable for the constitution of identity (of an individual or an ego).[1] In response to this unrepresentable longing, we have only substitutes: the ego ideal, God, the leader, as well as "father" in all the senses of the word.

Of course, Freud knows, as we all do, that longing—nostalgia—tends toward the unattainable, not to say the impossible. The Greek root of *nostalgia* (composed of "home" and "ache") alludes to the pain of an impossible return. The German word refers to an obsessive tension for which there is no release. Freud's expression says it all: the Father did not take place. It is not his place to exist, even though his role or his figure is necessary. Although Freud never says this explicitly, he often comes very close to suggesting it. If the Father does not exist, the constitution of any group structured as a hierarchy—in the strongest sense of the term: an archaic sacrality—is based on an artificial substitution. On principle, society organizes itself around a substitution of its own principle.[2] In other words, society is essentially an-archic.[3]

If society is anarchic and is, inevitably, always threatened or haunted by dispersion or dissociation, we must ask how the slightest association is possible. Freud dealt with this question in *Group Psychology and the Analysis of the Ego, Totem and Taboo, Civilization and Its Discontents, Moses and Monotheism*, as well as in other texts from time to time. It was one of his major preoccupations after 1921 (the year that the first of these books was published).

In the title *Group Psychology and the Analysis of the Ego*, we should note the use of the coordinating conjunction, which indicates not simply a co-ordination but, indeed, a reciprocal implication. The question of groups must be connected to the ego, which in turn cannot be dissociated from that of groups. Moreover, a chiasmus can be seen here: psychology more obviously applies to the ego, while applying it to groups can seem a hazardous proposition. As for the analysis of the ego—that is, its psychoanalysis—it must take the group into account. How one element is transformed by the other is what the book aims to work out. Its intention is nothing less than to examine how the group and the ego, seemingly opposed, and even mutually exclusive, are, in fact, part of each other.

The longing for the Father—its inanity as well as its persistence—will be shown to be what drives this double and interminable movement, in regard to which the Mother, on the contrary, will reveal herself to be the space in which it unfolds.

2

The group (or the crowd), as Freud uses the term introduced by Le Bon, is distinct from "race" or from "a people."[4] The latter is based on heredity and on what is inherited; it produces a civilization or a culture, and therefore customs, traditions, etc. The group or the horde, on the other hand, is a gathering not based on common origins but created by a situation, or it is a distinct organization within a nation, although it is a part of it (like the army or the Church). The horde is not constituted based on a specific origin; it arises spontaneously or arbitrarily, but it is not "indigenous" in the literal sense.

This distinction is at the heart of the problem: how does a group take shape without a given origin or identity? That is, how did the first human group come into existence? This questioning led Freud to study totemic societies, where he found signs of the constitution of a people on the basis of what he had defined as a primary relationship with a hidden origin. A totem is always an ancestor: it designates or figures the ancestor. A group does not know its ancestor, nor can it designate or represent him.

In more precise terms, a group is an entity whose creation or origin is simultaneous with the very figuration of an ancestral origin. In *Massenpsychologie*, Freud's reasoning makes its way toward this co-originarity.

In the process, he must deal with the question of the individuals composing the group. To be more exact, it is a question of understanding how individuals can compose something between themselves. Freud struggles to elucidate how this problematic composition is possible. From the point of view of the individual or the ego, this composition is excluded if the ego is characterized in terms of its self-sufficiency. From the collective perspective, the composition is opaque if the group is merely the coagulation, as it were, of individual units with no distinctive features. Indeed, the group reveals all kinds of erasures of individual autonomy.

In short, Freud reexamines the question of what Kant called "*unsociable sociability.*" Schopenhauer illustrated it using the fable of the porcupines quoted in *Massenpsychologie VI*.[5] It is indeed the question at the heart of the entire sociopolitical reflection of modernity: how is it possible to build a society?

3

In Freudian terms, and taking into account the book published two years later—*The Ego and the Id*—we can say that the question comes to be how an ego detaches itself from the id, and how, once it is detached, the ego can meet another ego. This formulation complicates the question, which now not only involves the presumption of an autonomous individual but also questions the origin of this individual, and thus his autonomy.

In all the previously mentioned texts, Freud strives to relativize or to reduce this autonomy. The ego is never completely separate from the id (like the conscious from the unconscious). It is, after all, only its "surface." There are several egos that all communicate with an id which seems to belong to each of them and is, at the same time, shared by all of them. The central question in *Massenpsychologie* concerns what Freud calls identifications, that is, the possibilities of communication (of contagion, of hypnotic relation) not associated with an object but with a relation (or a contact, a suggestion) between egos who perceive each other as similar. There is a sameness of egos (a sameness of selves) which makes identification possible.

Here, we can venture to add a comment to Freud's argumentation, about the double meaning of the word "identification." Aside from "putting oneself in the place of another," identification can mean the constitution and definition of one's own identity. Is it conceivable that an ego can only separate and become distinct if it identifies with another? This is the question that must be answered.

4

As it happens, the id has certain characteristics that could help us arrive at an answer.

The id, borrowed from Groddeck, originates in its turn from Nietzsche's *Selbst*.[6] This is not a "self" (*sich*) but a "same" related to itself, which is different because "self" does not contain the idea of the same. At the same time, the *Selbst*, as Freud wrote in a posthumous note, is endowed with a *Selbstwahrnehmung*, a perception of itself that is no doubt obscure but through which a sameness as such is perceived.

In other words, we can say that the id considers itself a locus of possible identities, that is, of distinctions between same and same—since it has within itself the aspect of the *Selbst*. In other words, the pre-individual is not simply or uniformly the same in every case: it contains, as its very structure, the potential of giving birth to egos which cannot individualize without incorporating in their individuality something of the sameness that generated them. And this something is the possibility of a relation with the same. To put it differently: to become my-*self* [*moi*-même], I pass through the perception of the other itself, the other same [*l'autre même*]. I use the word "perceptions" here as Freud used it in the expression "internal perceptions."[7] They designate "the most diverse and certainly also the deepest strata of the mental apparatus." The best example is the dyad pleasure-unpleasure. The notion of diversity refers to the various modalities or qualities that might be involved (how can there be pleasure or unpleasure, acceptance or refusal, assimilation or destruction). The notion of depth refers to the id or to the unconscious.

In *Massenpsychologie VIII*, when Freud makes a graphic representation of "egos that have put one and the same object [the 'guide'] in the place of their ego ideal and have consequently identified themselves with one another in their ego," the result, he says, is a "primary group."

The initial constitution of the group requires preestablished communication between those who form it. This communication cannot be limited to object relations, that is, to the libido. It must take place between subjects—not as a pact between constituted subjects but at the same time as they are being constituted. This was at bottom what Rousseau was intimating when he said that the social contract was at the same time a way of acceding to humanity. Indeed, the well-known paradox that asks how non-humans can enter into a contract—as symbolic an act as can be imagined—is illustrated by Freud through the difficulty of establishing simultaneity and anteriority between individuals and the group. This is the problem raised by identification, a problem Freud admits he does not know how to solve satisfactorily.

5

It is out of the question to claim to solve a dilemma that doubtless cannot be solved—although the question concerns nothing less than the raison d'être of humanity as a species of "political animal." The capacity of humans to live together—with their passions and language—is in itself enigmatic. It is not a given. Aristotle's expression means not only "a species properly suited to live in a city-state" but, above all, a species whose proper nature it is to assemble in debate and to choose the modalities of coming together in a community. In Aristotle, this is called a "species endowed with *logos*."

Language in fact has a remarkable role to play in Freud with respect to the formation of the group. In section B of the postscript of *Group Psychology*, the murder of the father of the primitive horde is presented as a fictional tale told by one of the children to the others. This child is presumably the youngest and, as such, the mother's favorite, the one she protected from the father. This does not prevent the privileged son from feeling deprived of the father, and he separates himself from the group (the group exists but lacks structure).[8] What the son feels is nostalgia for the primal father.

We can rephrase this by saying: the inventor of the first story of the origin wants to invent himself as the murderer of the father, that is, as the one who has replaced him. He is impelled to do this by nostalgia, a *Sehnsucht* which, being a *Sucht*, has the character of an addiction or a passion—the passionate desire Freud distinguishes in a group.[9] Thus, he is driven by a double affect: this passionate nostalgia and his mother's unique tenderness. This leads him to create a "fictitious re-interpretation of the time of the origins." He invents a myth and becomes its mythical hero. By narrating his fictional poem of the invention of the origin, he allows the others to identify with him, because they all feel the nostalgia for the father. "The myth, then, is the step by which the individual emerges from group psychology."

He emerges from it to confirm its truth, we might say. For the myth introduces the very possibility of identification. The group identifies with the hero, and thereby identifies itself as an aggregate of similar identities, which are therefore interchangeable or replaceable. Here, Freud's note refers the reader to a book by Hanns Sachs.[10] Reading Sachs, it becomes clear that Freud has relied on his analysis of heroization. However, there is one assertion of the text that Freud overlooked. Hanns Sachs ends his description of the poet as hero of the tale by noting that identifying him (in the sense of recognizing him) could prevent his listeners from identifying with the hero. "To avoid this obstacle, the poet must create an impersonal hero or, to be more precise, a superpersonal hero with whom he can identify, as can all his listeners, since he is at once all of them and none of them."

Freud neglected this assertion because he remained focused on the figure of the dominant hero, who becomes God or the leader. In his view, identification is primarily, and even essentially, hierarchical.[11] He subordinates to it the horizontal identification that is nonetheless necessary to the primary one—which does not necessarily mean anterior but at least concomitant. The longing for the father preoccupies him, while he explores the question of how egos that are forming—separating from the id and among themselves [*entre eux*]—also recognize each other as kindred.

6

It would not be amiss for us to review more attentively the conditions Freud himself defined for setting in motion the process of identification. These two conditions are language and affect. Let us look at each one before examining the relation between them.

Obviously, language constitutes not only the means but the actual location of identification, whether it be that of the son with the father or that of brothers with the hero created by one of them. We must indeed speak of creation here, since it is out of nothing that the father is invented, that is, named. This naming at the same time gives him his own proper name—be it simply "Father" as the name of one who has neither name nor existence—and gives the name of the genesis or generation which produced the group. The latter identifies with an unidentifiable identity. The group or the collectivity is the entity which searches for an identity, or projects one. It is what awaits or demands an identity, that is, a *Selbst* for itself, because the "itself" is what is obscurely perceived as inherent to the existence of anything whatever—of all physical or physiological bodies, of all entangled or heaped-together presences.

Language does not respond to this demand: it exposes it as a demand; it exposes the general quest for the identical within an indistinct and indefinite multiplicity. But it remains language insofar as it bears the possibility of identifying what we call a sense; or, we might also turn this around and say: insofar as sense is an element of identity and of distinction, which is its corollary.

Freud presents a similar hypothesis when he formulates a myth of the birth of the myth, which is precisely the birth of language and/or sense. Lacan understood correctly that this is what lies at the heart of the matter. He designated identification as "identification of the signifier"[12] and made it clear at once that it is not "imaginary identification," meaning that it is not identification with a given form or figure but rather mutual identification between two (or more) entities discovering each other as "same" in their very capacity to form a form not given, in other words, their capacity to signify.

Indeed, it is here that it becomes most clear that Lacan's "signifier" should be understood in the active form, as the subject in the act of signifying—or of producing meaning (a subject being, in fact, precisely this capacity or this signifying promptness). This capacity is the same in all subjects, and because it functions one instance at a time, on each occasion when meaning arises, it also explains why, as Lacan says: "the speaking subject always ends up taking you for another." This relation to another, existing between all "same" entities, is what Lacan has named the "big Other"; but we could also say that it is the relation of sense, which is, each time, relation *to* sense as that which, at the same time, distinguishes and ties together selves (egos, in fact, but egos in the process of identifying themselves and each other, and never "identified" egos, as when using the past participle).

The Lacanian interpretation resolves Freud's dilemma perfectly: it sheds light on the communication of strictly distinct egos which, having originated in the same id, still belong to it after separating into "same" entities that signify to each other their shared discretion and discreteness—that is, in the mathematical sense of the word but also in the sense of "reserve," of restraint shown by each one, which remains the other, as well as an altogether other, to borrow Derrida's expression.[13]

7

This logic of separate entities corresponds to Lacan's "unary trait": each one counts for one, and none counts for all.[14] But how then are we to understand the distinction—not very discrete this time—made for the favorite son, creator and hero of the myth?

As this hero, he is a poet, and Freud underscores the poetic nature of this first word. This may explain, to some degree, why he did not take into account Hanns Sachs's last assertion: even if the hero counts the same as all and as none, it was necessary to invent this "impersonal or rather superpersonal" figure. Freud was perhaps anticipating the superego that the inventor of the myth could bring into being or himself become. In this context, we should expand on the notion of "archeophilia" alluded to earlier. The anarchy I spoke of probably cannot be smoothly separated from hierarchy. (As we know, this entanglement presents a problem for democracy.) But this is not what concerns us here. It is first of all the poet as such who is distinguished.[15] And as we know, Freud considers the poet to have a distinctive capacity. Here, it is illustrated by the "fictional tale," which relies on a talent or an art that is all the more special in that what is "reinterpreted"[16] has never been interpreted before (otherwise it would be necessary to attribute the invention of the myth to the father). The first poet invents a sense by hiding the previous sense—which supposes that there was one.

To do this, the poet is endowed with special qualities. For instance, he has "a sensitivity that enables them to perceive the hidden impulses in the minds of other people, and the courage to let his own unconscious speak."[17] The creator of the myth perceived the longing for the father in all the people, and by letting his unconscious speak he gave voice to the unconscious of all—a voice at once singular and plural, so that everyone communicates with everyone, in a sharing of communality. This communication is not *logos*, at least not Aristotle's *logos* functioning as a "political" faculty of communication about the common good. Or else it would be necessary to conjoin to this *logos*, and inextricably so, the *mythos*, whose primary value is not that of discourse but of expression, of declaration. While the *logos* discusses, the *mythos* proclaims. It is a *saying* invested in its own *said*, or, put differently, *it is a saying* which, before all else, *says itself*. We could even go so far as to designate it as a *so-called saying* [un soi-disant dire], a saying that calls up its own supposed saying, that says itself as saying.

8

By saying itself, it communicates to others this self-saying [*cette soi-disance*]. Myth is speech that is proper to all and to each one, while the *logos* is a discourse for all but proper to no one. They stand back to back, a *Janus geminus* of language rooted in the id and articulated by egos.

Thus, the poet is the other of the logician (learned man, philosopher, orator). He is the other who speaks of the same thing, specifically, of the being-together, the *Mitsein* that sustains language, which in turn sustains the *Mitsein*. But if there should be an internal division of language itself, what would it consist of? Obviously, the *logos* relates to the separated ego, while *mythos* relates to the id from which an ego is in the process of emerging. Therefore, the proximity between poetry and psychoanalysis approaches intimacy. Still, intimacy is not identity, just as identification is not unification.

Lacan knew it very well, and did not stop at recognizing the same proximity as Freud but went as far as identifying himself—or rather his speech, or himself as a speaking being—as a poem.[18] By saying "I am not a poet but a poem," he identifies himself as speech at the origin, that is, speech as fertile ground, while rejecting what Bataille called the sticky temptation of poetry which, perhaps since Rimbaud, is constantly denounced: poetry as precious, grandiloquent aestheticism.[19] Taking this step seems to lead to identifying psychoanalysis with poetry. But Lacan only took this step playfully. He knew that the decision cannot be personal, because it would have to be set off initially by the mother and the group.

As we have seen, this setting off requires certain conditions. These are not necessarily absent today, and there are poets—in any case, there are poems—among us, although the conditions are not those of a Homer or a Shakespeare, to name two dubious egos which carry an indisputable power of identification whose effects live on.

We can therefore say: "poetry and psychoanalysis bring *Knowledge* into question, in order to arrive at the truth in their practice."[20] And we must add that it is precisely this act that philosophy has confronted or tried to carry out since Hegel up until today, that Lacan was able to reexamine, and that Freud introduced by asserting that the drives are "our myths." Nevertheless, we must ask ourselves why there are three contenders for a role which clearly requires unicity.

9

Unicity—even isolation—of the youngest son is, in fact, necessary for enabling the myth to address itself to each one and to everyone at the same time. A single voice must be heard by all who are alike. (Fascism, be it national-racial or techno-global, is nothing more than the forced artificial production of a single voice.)

Indeed, what isolates the youngest son, what pre-individualizes him, we might say, is first that he is the last born, who closes the series, and second that he is the mother's favorite. She no doubt prefers him precisely because he closes the series. It is as if the father's fertility, or the mother's, has come to an end, or as if the mother in any case wanted it to end (and therefore as if, in a sense, the father's role has started to decrease). The youngest is thus the object or the subject of two powerful affects: the love of the mother and the hatred of the father.

This double affect is affection itself, with the ambivalence it implies. Affection not only comes from outside the subject: it shapes him and is that through which he shapes the world (colors it, makes it vibrate). The mother's love is precisely this: coming into the world. For this reason, the mother is never completely distinct from the world (or from the id) and for the same reason she can be rejected as well as loved, since being in the world also means no longer being the world itself, with its indistinct identity.

By contrast, the father is detachment itself: he is the possibility of an outside-the-world, of autonomy. Therefore, he is hated in two ways: as an expulsion into the world,[21] very different from a bringing into the world, and at the same time, as the self-sufficient position that can only serve as an "ego ideal" to an ego which separates or aspires to separation.

This double affective duplicity, this redoubling between mother and father of the ambivalence which, essentially, is affect itself—the push propelling toward detachment, toward individuality—forces us to step back from Freud or to expand on him in order to recognize that it is the same impulse: that of the id. The obscure self-perception of the id can only perceive at the same time a form of sameness to self and the drive or impulse of this form toward itself, that is, toward its separating off as an "ego."

The id and the ego are so closely interrelated that not only is the ego driven to separate but this impulse is also that of the id. This being so, the ego can only continue to be rooted in the id, and the id can only persist in the ground of the ego. In that case, the longing for the father must be understood as an objective and subjective genitive: longing for the father *and* paternal longing for the ego, in which it wants to see itself reflected. Applying this to narcissism: since absolute narcissism cannot exist (these terms are contradictory), we must turn to relative narcissism—that which is at work in the relation, or narcissism which is itself relational.

If we were to pursue this reasoning, we would see how the mother and the father are intertwined, or how thrownness and being-in-the-world are correlated, as well as how this correlation involves the collective or plurality of egos, since on the father's side there can only be exclusion of unicity, and on the mother's side there is the world, which supposes alterity and the circulation of distinct elements of meaning. And on both sides, there is affective ambivalence: love and hate of what threw me forth and of what opened the world to me.

10

Affectivity, as we have said, does not happen to the subject: it stirs him and therefore moves him. As Simondon wrote: "Affectivity-emotivity is a movement between the naturally indeterminate and the *hic et nunc* of present existence."[22] Existence which is therefore seen as "incorporated in the collective," since "the individual as experiencer is a connected being."

At this point, we must agree with Lacan's assertion: "The collective is nothing other than the *subject* of the individual."[23] This must, of course, be understood based on the nature of the Lacanian subject, whose "existence is that of an 'in-between,' he belongs to a *mesology*."[24] The collective is at the same time what we might call the natural milieu of the individual, and the relational space in which individuals form relations with each other. They mutually experience each other as long as they are moved: no matter how small the emotion, it is what sets in motion the egos *between them*.

What happens to language in this movement? Freud does not say—although he is careful to point out the "cap of hearing" of the ego.[25] In Lacan's view, language changes affect into "another thing." "It transforms it, through speech, into a means of communication."[26] Yet, since affect already exists in the relation with the other, it is not enough to speak of this displacement—which Lacan sees as metaphor understood precisely as displacement (the Greek meaning of the word) from the literal to the figurative, or from inexpressible fantasy to communicable speech.[27]

If we stopped there, we would not give any reason for this supposed metaphorization. We must go farther in our examination of the relation between language and affect. Rousseau has opened the way. We know that he said: "needs dictated the first gestures, and the passions wrung the first utterings [*voix*]."[28] Affect produces speech, or more exactly, it first makes the voice ring out.[29] This is not articulated language at first but rather the acoustic aspect of what Bernard Baas calls "the sonorous body": the voice insofar as it is part of the body, coming from it and formed in it.

What is formed in this way takes the body outside itself. It lets it be heard. This hearing is a sensing: Rousseau says the voice modulates "the accents of passion" and "these accents make us quiver [. . .] make us feel what we hear." Through the voice, the body communicates with the body of the other. This communication knows nothing of the transposition of the inexpressible into expression: it creates a link, it is at the same time discovery of the other—of self as other, of the other as self, *the same*—and appeal to the other.[30] The primacy of the collective over the individual depends on this, that the appeal to "you" is contemporaneous with the separation of "I."

This appeal communicates an emotion only because the emotion itself is an appeal from the outside, and is outwardly directed—an actual setting in motion of the *same*. At the same time, there is no clearer instance of the nature of identification, revealing it as neither fusion nor unification. Emotion does not lead back to the id but is much more the *self-perception of the id addressing itself*.

It addresses itself and as soon as it does, it is altered and it identifies itself.

11

This is what makes it poetic. The poem is not first of all a bringing into play of language at the extreme edges of signification. It is, rather, the opening onto the possibility of meaning. Jean-Christophe Bailly wrote: "it is here [...] that is hidden—and from here that springs the sonic nature of the poem and its inborn relation to prosody and to song: the poem invents nothing, but by intersecting with language in this manner it gathers its *full resonance, and makes of this resonance the intensity of a sense. The poem is the tonality of sense.*"[31]

Suffice it to add that sense is above all tonality—tension, vibration, inflexion, not simply of the voice as an acoustic phenomenon but of the voice as affected body. Sense consists in this, that there is appeal and response. It is not signification, which on its own endlessly refers to other significations. It is, rather, this reference itself as an appeal to the other.

Sense is not beyond signification: it is the meaning-making in all signification insofar as it is always yet to come [*encore à venir*]. And in the body [*en corps*], it echoes the homophony that Baas makes resonate. Sense comes by way of the other and as other, it comes as the self-alteration of the id. A self-alteration indeed—coordinated with self-perception—since the voice is *heard*, it *hears itself*. Referring to Valéry's "Narcissus Speaks," Derrida commented that the voice "seems to do without the detour through the exteriority of the mirror or the water, the world, in order immediately to reflect itself in the intimate instantaneousness of resonance."[32]

This is how the poem, while letting its voice resonate for its own sake, without any intention to communicate, also gives voice not only to emotions but to the motion or pulsation of the world. "Religion is the oldest of all poems," Kant wrote.[33] Here, religion is not a faith, it is the calling out and listening to a voice that is the voice of all as it traverses a body—a totemic body, a mythical body which at the same time is no less that of a singular voice. It is the narration of the myth of the tribe.[34]

It can happen that a group does not find its myth, or loses it. In that case, it starts to decompose, its poets are poets in name only, for appearances, and the world becomes mere connection. But when there is real poetry (not Lacan's Pouasie), it gives voice not only to all[35] but to the cosmos—which is also in the id. The longing for the father, as the double genitive suggests, is the longing of the subject for a world, and the longing of the world for those who inhabit it. Poetry is the voice brought into the world, and the world brought into voice.

The same notion is expressed in Michel Deguy's verses, where "identification" has the sense of an assimilation into identity, and is contrasted with the similarity of sames:

La comparaison entretient l'incomparable
La distinction des choses entre elles
Poésie interdit l'identification
Pour la douceur du comme rigoureuse
Commun?
Comme-un
C'est tout comme si
C'était comme-un.[36]

Comparison sustains the incomparable
The distinction between things
Poetry forbids identification
Preferring the softness of the rigorous "like"
In common?
Alike
It is as if
It was alike.

MARCH 2021
—Translated by Agnès Jacob

Lesson

There is no doubt nothing more difficult to learn than the dividing up of our solitudes, since the first one is as essential to us as the ones that follow from it. Each one of us emerges from the same ground as everyone—and this ground is conjoined with all that lives, which is conjoined with the cosmos, with all that is and with the fact that there is all this [*tout ça*]. But each emergence effects a rupture without remainder: each individual is an absolute, distinct and separated-from-all, and bound to all others in their indistinction. As a speaking animal, the human individual manifests as such this exorbitant conjunction of separation and connection. At the heart and in the hollow of language, there is this insignificance—this non-signifying moment—of our common condition.

We do not cease enveloping our insignificance in all sorts of significations, justifications, and destinations. The slightest encounter, however, between us, as between us and all there is, does not fail to attest to its improbable, uncertain, risky, and dangerous character, which is no less charged with the integral and happy possibility of sense.

This contradiction is on display before us today as if, having exhausted every means of subtracting sense from its insignificance, we had decided to hand over to a great mad autonomous machine (autonomous, therefore mad) that which infinitely exceeds us. We have before us, and we feel already, a cruelty, ours, ready to sacrifice us to our own insignificance. Not turning our gaze away is our only chance, without it being given to us to know from which direction *it* is falling.

April–August 2021

All my gratitude goes to Cécile Bourguignon and to Hélène Nancy for their attentive rereadings and for their suggestions.

—Translated by Jeff Fort

PART II

Stoma

Hymne Stomique

chant premier

Fille du Souffle et de la Chère,
père exhalé, mère absorbée
en toi par toi dans ta trouée
comme le veut l'ordre des choses
mâle aspiré dans les nuées,
femelle sucée avalée,

toi passage dedans dehors
en haut en bas et leurs mêlées,
leur brassage leur masticage
—*Mastax* fut de ta parenté—
toi la mêleuse la brouilleuse
souveraine des amalgames
amal al-djam'a al-modjam'a
ou *malagma* du malaxer
toujours l'un qui dans l'autre passe
en transmutation d'alchymie

toi la parleuse la mangeuse
la discoureuse la buveuse
la clameuse la dévoreuse

salut, Stoma commissures humides

Stoma: A Hymn

first song

Daughter of Breath and Dear Delicious Face,
father exhaled, mother absorbed
in you by you in your gaping hole
as called for by the order of things
male sucked up into swarming cloud,
female sucked swallowed,

you passage inside and out
from top to bottom and their mixings,
their immixture their mastication
—*Mastax* being one of your common roots—
you the mixer the masher[1]
sovereign of amalgamations
amal al-djam'a al-modjam'a
or *malagma*, from the word for blending [*malaxer*]
always one into the other slipping
in alchymic transmutation

you the speaker the eater
the chatterer the drinker
the shouter the devourer

salut, Stoma humid joining

rejointes disjointes
viande en *logos, mythos* en bave

salut, toi seule véritable
seule réelle dialectique!

of lips disjointed
meat in *logos*, *mythos* in drooling

salut, you the only true
the only real dialectic!

chant deuxième

Tu avales et tu consommes:
tout en toi est programmé
à se faire consumer cailler coaguler concasser

tout réduit en gouttelettes
de sang de lymphe et de mucus
tout dégluti digéré
ingéré égrugé trituré transfusé dissout
le reste à l'autre bouche évacué

légume fruit fromage rave corps et sang réincarnés
en protéines en farines vitamines et soupes sanguines
intimes et infimes
flots nourrissant la faim
celle qui s'ouvre en toi
celle qui s'aiguise par toi

la faim l'appétit le désir
la demande l'attente l'envie
la soif l'attraction l'espérance
quête enquête requête opiniâtre

tout ce qui fait couler ta salive lascive
s'entrouvrir de fièvre tes lèvres

tout ce qui t'ouvre la gueule
qui fait de tes dents la meule
du moulin et du four de cuisson et coction

second song

You swallow and you consume
everything finds itself in you
consumed curdled clotted crushed

all broken down to droplets
of blood of lymph and of mucus
all swallowed digested
ingested gristled fiddled transfused dissolved
all the rest through that other mouth evacuated

vegetable fruit cheese root body and blood reincarnated
in proteins in flours vitamins and blood red soups
intimate and frail
flux nourishing famished
that hunger which opens in you
which sharpens its edge through you

hunger appetite desire
demand wait want
thirst attraction hope
quest inquiry obdurate request

all that sets your lascivious saliva flowing
opens so slightly your feverish lips

all that opens your maw
that turns the teeth wet in your jaw
to stone for the mill and to stone for the stove[2]

chant troisième

Saluons à présent tes filles
Os et Bucca tes avatars
échos de ta profondeur

sanctuaire du dire et du goût conjugués
même orifice ouvrant l'antinomie
du flux et du jusant
de l'appel et de l'appétit

Os et Bucca sœurs jumelles
une hittite une celtique
latinement sororisées

les deux bords de ta béance
les deux lèvres les deux mâchoires
vestibule et cavité
résonnant de dedans à dehors
de dehors aérien à dedans viscéral

l'esprit et la matière la matière et l'esprit
l'un à l'autre abouchés comme d'un long baiser
que chaque lèvre avec l'autre partage
matière impénétrable esprit pénétrant tout
jusqu'à son incapacité à pénétrer le fond

mais au fond se formant de la bouchée copieuse
pour s'élever jusqu'à la mordante denture

third song

Let us now greet your daughters
Os and *Bucca* your avatars
echoes of your depths

sanctuary of speech and taste conjoined
single orifice opening anatomy
of flux and of ebbing
of appeal and of appetite

Os and *Bucca* twin sisters
one Hittite one Celtic
Latinized sororitized

the twin rims of your yawning gap
two lips two jaws
vestibule and cavity
resonating outward from within
from airy outside to visceral inside

mind and matter matter and mind
the one and the other pressing mouths together as in a long kiss
that each lip shares with the other
impenetrable matter mind penetrating all
right down to its inability to penetrate the ground [*le fond*]

but at bottom forming itself from this hearty mouthful
raising itself up to biting teeth

chant quatrième

Bucca se change en Os comme du même au même
et la voix retentit dans l'haleine et l'effluve

l'antre introductif de matière
émet un cri une gueulante
de souffrance de jouissance
d'appel de menace d'éclat

plainte de la bête blessée
verge érigée braillant son rut
vierge en pleurs vulve effarée
enfant qui réclame le lait
baleine qui clame en extase

voix que tu formes que tu lances
brame aboiement hululement braiment
un qui mugit un qui blatère
un qui jappe glapit mugit barrit vagit
criaille ou râle et piaule et roucoule gloussant

Stoma comme tu vocifères!
comme tu fouilles les peaux les cuirs tous les plumages
pour de chacun tirer un timbre une modulation
un rythme une cadence des accents tons et inflexions

comme tu joues des poumons des gosiers par espèces et genres
à chacune à chacun donnant son expression sa résonance inimitable

fourth song

Bucca becomes *Os* as same changes into same
and voice resounds in breath and emanation

introductory cavern of matter
lets loose a piercing cry
of suffering of enjoyment [*jouissance*]
of appeal of threat of fragment

complaint of the wounded beast
erected cock howling its heat
weeping virgin frightened vulva
infant crying for milk
whale crying out in ecstasy

voice that you form that you release
bellow bark wail bray
one who yawps one who bays
one who yips yelps yawps trumpets whines
whimpers or moans and chirps and clucking coos

how you vociferate, Stoma!
how you pass and probe skins leathers all the feathers
to draw from each a timbre a nuance
a rhythm a cadence accents tones and inflections

how you play with lungs and with throats through species and genus
to each and every giving its expression and resonance that no other can
render

chant cinquième

et puis un son qui vaut un sens
desserre les dents d'un grand singe
en lui défripant la méninge

la voix y perd son ton y trouve la parole
ô mots articulés phonation laborieuse
cordes tendues par un désir de dire
de montrer faire voir annoncer sans toucher sans nulle présence
évoquer

modulation de l'absence
et d'abord de l'absence d'un sens
tant sont les langues nombreuses et chacune son sens chacune sa voix
secrète
bouche plurielle
aux embouchures dispersées sur l'océan du sens

le sens se noie il danse sur les vagues
il écume infiniment
son écume sa profusion sa débauche sa luxuriance
son recommencement toujours

de bouche à oreille un secret circule
voix de personne à tous et chacun adressée
sans jamais s'épuiser ni jamais se résoudre
sans avoir commencé ni pouvoir finir et jamais un dernier mot

ou bien chaque mot peut faire une fin

comme chaque fois la bouche se ferme

fifth song

and then a sound that is worthy of sense
loosens a great ape's lips
smoothing out his gray matter

the voice loses its tone and finds its speech
oh articulated words laborious phonation
chords drawn taut by a desire to say
to show to describe to announce without touching without presence
evoking

a modulation of absence
first and foremost of the absence of a sense
such is the multiplicity of languages each with its meaning to each its
secret voice
plural mouth
whose mouths lead out into the ocean of sense

sense is swallowed up it dances on the waves
foaming infinitely
its froth its profusion its debauchery its luxuriance
its ever-renewed beginning-again

from mouth to ear a secret circulates
no one's voice addressed to each and all
without ever finding itself exhausted or settled
without having begun nor being able to end and never a last word

or each word can mark an ending

as each time the mouth closes[3]

LA BOUCHE RÉPOND

Je vous entends, je vous entends
Flatteurs
Qui feignez d'ignorer mes douleurs
D'ignorer que je suis déchirée
Outrée outragée meurtrie
Par vos vociférations de souffrance ou d'assurance
Vos clameurs hilares braillardes
Vos discours harangues palabres sermons hourvaris bavardages

C'est un de vos philosophes qui dit:

Dans les grandes occasions la vie humaine
se concentre encore bestialement dans la bouche, la colère fait grincer les dents, la
terreur et la souffrance atroce font de la bouche l'organe de cris déchirants.

Hegel lui-même oui
Hegel qui gueule
Convoquant grandes occasions pour m'y montrer bestiale
Bestiale l'embouchure même
de votre humanité
bestiale la douleur qui me déchire
non seulement quand vous hurlez
mais aussi lorsque vous chantez

lorsque vous m'étirez les lèvres
à rompre leurs commissures
à les changer en blessures
pour lancer des trilles aigus
des aboiements amoureux
dans vos opéras fameux

vous oubliez le supplice
que c'est de devoir mâcher
et remâcher
la chair dure de vos délices

et l'étreinte du baiser
savez-vous qu'elle m'étouffe
et que sa baveuse esbroufe

THE MOUTH RESPONDS

I hear you, I hear you
Flatterers
Who pretend to ignore my pains
To ignore that I am torn asunder
Offended outraged bruised
By your vociferations of suffering or assurance
Your loudmouth hilarious clamorings
Your speeches harangues parables sermons racket chatter

It was one of your philosophers who said:

On important occasions human life
is still centered in the mouth, anger makes the teeth
gnash, atrocious
terror and suffering turn the mouth into the organ of piercing screams.[4]

Hegel himself yes
Hegel who shouts
Conjuring up important moments to make me look bestial
Bestial the very mouthpiece
of your humanity
bestial the pain that tears me apart
not only when you scream
but also when you sing

when you pull apart my lips
far enough to rip their corners
to turn them into wounds
for throwing out sharp trills
amorous barkings
in your famous operas

you forget the torment
that is having to chew
and chew again
the hard flesh of your delicacies

and the embrace of the kiss
do you know how it smothers me
and how its drool-heavy bluff

jamais ne sut m'apaiser

Je vous entends faiseurs d'hymnes
Vous me bourrez de vos amphigouris et de leurs gargarismes
Gonflant mes joues exténuant ma langue
assurés que ça résonne alors que ça me bâillonne

....

never knew how to appease me

I hear you makers of hymns
You stuff me full of your amphigories and their garglings
Swelling my cheeks extenuating my tongue
Assured that it resonates whereas it gags me

•••••••••••••••••••••••••••••••••••••••

chant sixième

non imparfaites les langues en cela que plusieurs
ni accomplies mais mobiles vivantes
mortes aussi parfois non déchiffrées
idiomes silencieux

la langue dans la bouche mobile et ductile
touche à tout vibre phonétique
frénétique

frémit trémule et palpite et tressaille
mollusque vif aux muscles souples
palpitation élocutoire

langue intime glissée dans la bouche comme un pain quotidien
baise moi des baisers de ta bouche
baiser de paix baiser volé baiser donné
élixir de ta bouche où l'amour se pavane

langue indomptable
langue lascive
langue qui lèche et qui lappe
battant de la cloche de chair
carillon de la glotte
charme charnu orné de la luette

caressante médisante
vipérine praline

langue tongue Zunge lengua
języcsek ulimi lugha
langue dans toutes les langues, langue toute dans toute langue

sixth song

not imperfect in that languages are many[5]
nor finished but mobile living
dead as well sometimes undeciphered
silent idioms

the tongue in the mouth mobile and ductile
touches everything vibrates phonetic
frenetic

shivers quivers and palpitates and trembles
living mollusk with supple muscles
elocutionary palpitation

intimate tongue slipped into the mouth like a daily bread
kiss me with your mouth's kiss [*baiser*]
kiss of peace stolen kiss kiss given
your mouth's elixir where love struts proud

tongue untamable
tongue lecherous
tongue that licks and laps
ringing the bell of the flesh
glottal carillon
decorative fleshy charm of the uvula

caressing slandering
forked salty-sweet

tongue *langue Zunge lengua*
języczek zycsek ulimi lugha
tongue in every language, each tongue in every other tongue

chant septième

chante bouche chante le chant bouleversant
le thrène et l'hymne et la complainte
l'aubade le lied le fado
chante la barcarolle et l'arioso
fredonne ritournelles
entonne goualantes mélopées barcarolles

de toi le chant s'échappe et chavire en touchant
des lointains éloignés plus que les galaxies

bouche qui chante fuit à l'infini
d'une flèche enchantée
dont le vol vibre et vrille l'inouï

chante le chant qui charme
cantilène cantate
cantique cavatine

la gorge en pâmoison
les lèvres étirées
l'air forçant le passage
l'expiration sans condition

ô chante bouche
d'un chant de sirène ou de cygne
d'une romance d'un murmure

seventh song

sing mouth sing that moving song
the threnody and the hymn and the lament
the *aubade* the *lieder* the *fado*
sing the gondolier's *barcarole* and the *arioso*
hum *ritornellos*
burst out into *goualante* ballads chants *barcaroles*

from you song escapes sways and rolls in touching
faraway spaces more remote even than galaxies

mouth that sings flees into infinity
on an enchanted arrow
whose flight pulses and pierces into the unheard-of[5]

sing the song that enchants
cantilena cantata
canticle *cavatina*

swooning throat
lips drawn taut
air forcing through
expiration without condition

oh sing mouth sing
of a siren's song or a swan's
of a romance or of a murmur

LA BOUCHE RÉPOND

Vous parlez de murmure comme d'une aventure
Légère et caressante et douce
Quand il est difficile et sévère et contraint
De serrer les lèvres à ne plus les décoller
Pour laisser frémir et vrombir
Le fond sans fond de ma gorge

Car c'est cela exactement cela que vous méconnaissez
Ou que vous voulez oublier
Cela le fond sans fond de ma belle ouverture
Traversée sans répit de dehors à dehors
De ciel à terre et de zéphyr à fumier
Qui ne fait lien que de passage
Outrepassage et trépassage
Dans le vrombissement d'une mouche
Qui touche
Au silence effrayant des espaces infinis

Sachez-le il est dur de n'avoir pas de fin

THE MOUTH RESPONDS

You speak of murmur as though of an adventure
Light and caressing and sweet
Whereas it is difficult and severe and constrained
To close one's lips so tight as to never unseal them
So that the bottomless depths of my throat
Can quiver and buzz

For that is exactly what you misunderstand
Or what you want to forget
That the bottom without bottom of my beautiful opening
Relentlessly traversed from outside to outside
From sky to earth and zephyr to dung heap
Who only makes a passing link
Passing-beyond and trespassing
In the fly's buzzing
That touches
On the terrifying silence of infinite spaces[7]

Know that it is hard not having an end

chant huitième

bouche suce bouche tète
aspire afflux de lait de sperme
émissions liqueurs humeurs
le corps entier liquéfié
fondu fusionné fuyant
liquation et libation
fluides humides coulures
épanchements affluences
ruisseaux rigoles goulottes
goulûment pompées abreuvées
cascades et cascatelles
sueurs suintements mouillures
vapeurs vagues moiteurs tièdes
salive salace et salée
coulée de l'âme énamourée
dégorgée déchargée
distillée débondée
déversée répandue
perdue
filée
défaite
laissée
pissée
lâchée
donnée
vidée
vannée
claquée
sucée

eighth song

mouth suck mouth suckle
inhale flood of milk of sperm
emissions liquors humors
the whole body liquified
faded fused fleeing
liquidation and libation
humid drippy fluids
pouring rushing out
trickles streams channels
greedily sucked watered
cascades large and small [*cascades et cascatelles*]
sweats seepings dampenings
vapors waves warm humidities
salacious and salty saliva
flow of the enamored soul
disgorged discharged
distilled unleashed
poured spread
lost
left
undone
left behind
pissed
let loose
given
emptied
exhausted [*vannée*]
clacked out [*claquée*][8]
sucked

chant neuvième

récitations

ouvre ma bouche au dieu

entrée d'Enfer des Anciens

o grande bouche honorée
qui d'un large repli retrousse tes deux bords

Mais toujours de mon cœur ma bouche est l'interprète

Do you remember—it seems to say—
The mouth that smiled, beneath your mouth,
And kissed you . . . Yesterday?

ô figue ô figue désirée
bouche que je veux cueillir

Il poeta non imita la natura: ben è vero che la natura parla dentro di lui e per la sua bocca

On entend d'une bouche en apparence humaine
Sortir des mots pareils à des rugissements

Je veux décoller ma bouche de celle des autres hommes

et cependant je sens ma bouche aller vers toi

si ma couleur a les lèvres charnues
c'est pour mieux embrasser l'horizon et son mépris

Quum dabit amplexus atque oscula dulcia figet,
Occultum inspires ignem, fallasque veneno.

Im Spiegel ist Sonntag,
im Traum wird geschlafen,
der Mund redet wahr.

Quand tu ouvres la bouche—ô Gul-i-siah—j'aperçois une caverne où s'alignent des perles dédaignées du tellal.

Fruit mûr à la chair ferme, sombres extases du vin noir, bouche qui fais lyrique ma bouche

ninth song

recitations

Open my mouth to god?[9]

the mouth of hell of the Ancients[10]

oh great and honored mouth
you who with a wide fold pulled up your two hems

But playing always interpreter for my heart, my mouth

Do you remember—it seems to say—
The mouth that smiled, beneath your mouth,
And kissed you . . . Yesterday?[11]

oh fig oh desired fig
mouth I want to pick [like a fruit]

Il poeta non imita la natura: ben è vero che la natura parla dentro di lui e per la sua bocca[12]

One hears coming out of an apparently human mouth
Words that resemble roars

I want to unstick my mouth from that of others [other men—*des autres hommes*]

and yet I sense my mouth going toward you

if my color has full fleshy lips
it is to better embrace the horizon and its contempt

Quum dabit amplexus atque oscula dulcia figet
Occultum inspires ignem, fallasque veneno[13]

Im Spiegel ist Sonntag,
im Traum wird geschlafen,
der Mund redet wahr.[14]

When you open your mouth—oh Gul-i-siah—I glimpse a cavern lined with pearls spurned by the *tellal*.[15]

Ripe fruit with firm flesh, black wine's dark ecstasies, mouth that makes my mouth lyric

chant dixième

récapitulation

Estomac vient de *stoma* comme vient de la bouche ce que nous digérons
et cela même remonte à la bouche en *stomargos* ou en *eustomos*
parler vif ou éloquent

Embouchures des fleuves
mêlées des eaux
douces salées
poissons anadromes
poissons catadromes

reflux des marées
mascaret remontant le fleuve

dégorgement baveux
vomissure crachat
bouche anale vaginale
bouche aux lèvres abouchée
bouchée de pain d'amour d'esprit
Chacune de ces bouchées que j'arrache à la réalité pour la livrer
    à la digestion spirituelle

bouche-à-bouche des amants
et celui des sauveteurs
salutaire ou salvatrice
Albertine glissait dans ma bouche, en me faisant le don de sa langue,
comme un don du Saint-Esprit

Il est un élément anatomique qui explique que la bouche ait tendance aux excès: c'est qu'en elle circulent à la fois les mets et les mots. Dans sa grande parcimonie, la nature a en effet donné à la langue la double fonction du parler et du mange. Un seul organe pour deux fonctions: voilà qui devrait signaler à l'homme qu'il doit gérer avec mesure à la fois ce qui entre et ce qui sort de sa bouche. Mais, dans sa grande imprudence, la nature a par là même fait de la bouche une dangereuse zone de transit, une porte d'entrée et de sortie, un carrefour où se croisent l'alimentaire et le verbal et où les risques d'accidents sont grands.

Bouche sur bouche et le flanc sur le flanc

tenth song

recapitulation

Stomach comes from *stoma*, just as all that we digest comes from the mouth and it even comes back up to the mouth in the form of *stomargos* or *eustomos* lively eloquent speech

Mouths of rivers
mixing of waters
fresh and salt
anadromous fish
catadromous fish

ebb and flow of tides
tidal bore heading upstream

slimy discharge
vomit spittle
anal vaginal mouth
mouth coupled to lips
morsel of bread of love of mind
Each of these morsels that I wrest from reality and serve up for
    spiritual digestion

the lovers' mouth-to-mouth
and that of paramedics
aid or salvation
Albertine slipped into my mouth, giving me the gift of her tongue as though it were a gift from the Holy Ghost

An anatomical aspect of the mouth doubtless helps explain its tendency toward excess: both food and word pass through it. In its great parsimoniousness, nature decided to give the tongue a double task, both speaking and eating. One organ for two roles: this alone should be enough to remind man to handle with caution both what goes into and what goes out of his mouth. Yet in its equally great thoughtlessness, in so doing nature also turned the mouth into a dangerous zone of transit, a port of both entry and exit, an intersection at which the alimentary and the verbal cross paths and where the risk of accident is quite high.

Mouth on mouth and side by side

Il n'y a pas de concept "je" englobant tous les je qui s'énoncent à tout instant dans les bouches de tous les locuteurs.

Ta bouche c'est le ciel même,
Mon âme veut s'y poser
Puisse mon souffle suprême
S'en aller dans ce baiser.

No concept of "I" exists which can encompass all the "I"s pronouncing themselves at any given moment in the mouths of every speaker.

Your mouth is heaven itself
My soul seeks to rest there
May my last breath
Take flight in this kiss.[16]

chant onzième et dernier

Stoma, c'est toi qui nous avales!
Stoma, c'est toi qui nous parles!

Nous ne sommes pas tes usagers
mais toi tu uses de nous
tu uses tu abuses

tu nous ouvres d'un bout à l'autre
du ciel jusqu'à la terre

avalant le premier fumant la seconde
et toujours parlant

toujours par toi parlés articulés pincés vibrés

sans toi serions vases clos
circuits fermés
avec toi
sommes ouverts et traversés
passages pour demande et incantation
pour métabole et sémantique
pour mélange de l'une et l'autre

par toi sommes troués pensés pulsés
exprimés exclamés emportés
dans la tempête de ta jouissance

eleventh and last song

Stoma, it is you who swallows us!
Stoma, it is you who speaks us!

We are not your users
but you, you use us
you use you abuse

you open us up from one end to the other
from on-high to down here on earth

swallowing the first smoking the second
and speaking always

always through you [we are] spoken articulated pinched vibrant

without you we would be closed vessels
closed circuits
with you
we are open and traversed
passages for making demands and incantations
for metabolas and semantics
for mixtures of one and the other

through you we are pierced thought pulsed
expressed exclaimed excited
in the tempest of your *jouissance*

LA BOUCHE RÉPOND

Je vous entends c'est vous qui jouissez
De moi
De ma voix de ma voie mon aloi mon envoi mon émoi mon qui mon quoi
Et de ma joie
C'est vous qui tressaillez

Par moi vous voici parlés
Par moi vous voilà chantés
Par moi baisés accolés liquidés
Entonnés loués secoués

On vous dit animaux doués du langage
Mais celui-ci vous vient de mon palais
Il descend d'un plus haut lignage
Que votre espèce douée d'idées de notions et d'expressions

Mon palais abrite un trésor de vibrations d'exclamations
De tremblements et de rebonds
Rumeurs tumultes et bourdons
Battues froissements harmonies
Geignements sanglots roucoulades
Bruits de fond de surface d'attaque
Modulations souffles et pâmoisons
Ressassements des toujours mêmes sons
En tons toujours variés

C'est moi qui vous alterne
Moi qui vous ébranle
Moi qui vous agite
Qui vous trouble
Vous remue vous ouvre et vous ferme

C'est moi qui vous balance et qui vous berce
C'est moi qui vous cadence et qui vous pense

Décembre 2020

THE MOUTH RESPONDS

I hear you it is you whose pleasure comes
From me
Of my voice of my path my alloy my envoy my emotion my who my what
And of my joy
It is you who shudders

Through me there you are spoken
Through me there you are sung
Through me kissed coupled liquidated
Bellowed praised shaken

They say you are animals endowed with language
But that comes to you from my palace [palais][17]
It comes down from a higher lineage
Than your species endowed with ideas of notions and expressions

My palace harbors a treasure of vibrations of exclamations
Of tremblings and of reverberations
Noises tumults and ringings
Hunts rustlings harmonies
Whimpers weepings whispers
Background noises of attack surfaces
Modulations breaths and swoonings
Ruminations of always the same sounds
In always varied tones

It is me who alternates you
Me who shakes you
Me who agitates you
Me who troubles you
Stirs you opens you and closes you

It is me who rocks you and cradles you
It is me who rhythms you and who thinks you

DECEMBER 2020
—*Translated by Robert St. Clair*

Afterword to *Stoma*

Andrea Gyenge and John Paul Ricco

For Jean-Luc in Memoriam

Cavernous and yawning, the mouth is an abyss, a border, a threshold, a no-man's-land.[1] At once the site of appetites, nourishment, and life, it also leads circuitously to shit, vomit, blood, and death. It seems almost too rich with symbolism, too infinite in its diverging drives and desires, to ever take the form of a proper object for critical inquiry. One gets the sense, therefore, that a poet would be a better devotee than a philosopher. One might be inclined to think that only a poet would know how to answer to the mouth's machinations of bone, flesh, speech, and scream. After all, the mouth is the home of poetic labor—there where song and meter meet sound and air to unravel the better designs of reason. Plato, who knew well the dangers of poetic practice, thus sought to keep the poet separate from the *polis* and from the philosopher kings who would shape its best and most just futures. A good philosopher would never be a poet; the good philosopher would never *want* to be a poet. Better to keep the mouth and its poetic falsehoods far from the interrogative speech of Socratic reason and its rigors of dialogue, and avoid a seduction by the passions, a slide into unknowing and dissimulation. And yet it is also Plato who, in *Laws*, described philosophy as "the most beautiful of poems."[2] Indeed, the question of the intimacy between philosophy and poetry is discussed by Jean-Luc Nancy most directly in an interview from 2003, during which he asks: "Aren't philosophy and poetry, from their shared birth, structured like a Mobius strip?"[3] Nancy argues that philosophy, but also and more importantly thinking, remains attracted to the lure of poetry, to what Georges Bataille described as its "sticky temptation."[4] This is because, as Nancy explains, "reason demands poetry. It demands its own excess. . . . Poetry . . . as the uncertain double—uneasy and disturbing, dependent on the moment—of critical reason."[5]

In *Hymne Stomique*, Nancy gives us the story that precedes the shared birth of philosophy and poetry. It is a story of the "first" as the recommencement of beginning, and it is a doubled genesis story: the birth of the stomatic opening that is also the birth of thinking. Stoma is one name for "an infinite self-antecedence of philosophy"[6] and poetry and all forms and modes of speech, voice, language, oral sound, and buccal noise.

Given in eleven songs, Nancy's poem is thus something of a scandal. It is perhaps the oldest possible scandal in the history of philosophy. Oldest because it carries the imprint of philosophy's violent founding in the rift between *mythos* and *logos;* a scar that inhabits the edge of both as memory of their exiled other. The poem's title immediately signals this Greek inheritance—songs (*hymnos*), yet here sung in praise of neither the gods, philosophy, nor poetry, but a "salut," to an archi-originary opening (*stoma*)—a corporeal, lyrical, and at times violent ecstasis. *Hymne Stomique* is a hymn sung in adoration to the original adoration, given that, as Nancy once wrote: "Adoration is addressed to what exceeds address . . . nothing other than a mouth . . . nothing but an open body . . . Bodies are adorations in all their openings."[7] *Hymne Stomique* thus tells us that in the beginning was not the word, not even the word "mouth" nor even the mouth itself, but instead in the beginning was simply the opening of an opening (*stoma*). Stoma (not *logos* or *mythos*)[8] was not only "in" the beginning, but *is* the beginning and thus is the engendering, offering, and donation of the beginning's infinite recommencement each time, just this once—another name for which is "existence." Rewriting Arendt's philosophy of beginning, for Nancy, natality is buccality.[9]

The mouth is the site of an originating intrusion, birth, and burst of presence, and thus "not a foundation, but an opening—a serration, a wound."[10] And yet, as Nancy stresses in *The Inoperative Community*, "the open mouth is not a laceration" as though the site of a cut into a preexisting interior (i.e., the face) but rather the scission and decision as the scene and very *spacing* of the recommencement of existence as that which always intrudes upon itself and thereby is exposed to the Outside (*that* addressee without proper address): "The opening of this scene . . . [is] that which cannot be received from elsewhere or reproduced from any model, since it is always beginning, 'each time.'"[11] In doing so, the stomatic "mouth would be the first image," and so "older than the face."[12]

Written in the last year of his life, *Hymne Stomique* is Nancy's exclamatory answer to a question we posed to him in the guise of an interview on themes of the mouth in his oeuvre. In his generous style, he agreed to the interview quickly and with enthusiasm. Our first question: "Why an 'epic' of the mouth? If you were to write it, what would this epic look like?" was provoked by a comment he made in the preface for the English translation of *Ego Sum* (2016) where he writes: "Since I wrote this book, the mouth is the other motif that never leaves me, even though I have not written much more about it, as if I was waiting (but who, 'I'?) for a special occasion, the sudden discovery of the opportunity for an epic of the mouth."[13] In response to our question, Jean-Luc wrote back to say that the only way to answer was to write the epic itself. Within a matter of days, he sent us the eleven-song *Hymne Stomique*, followed a few days later by a second draft that now included the three sections in which "the mouth responds." In retrospect, we now understand that our question was not truly a question but an invitation to that "special occasion"—as if that text was waiting for us (but who, "us"?) to bring itself into being. Even though we are scholars of Nancy's work and intimately familiar with the breathtaking gestures of his thought, we are still stunned by what he returned to us. In the wake of his death, the existence of this poem feels precarious and fragile—as if it is shot through with the retreat of a body that was failing but still dancing joyously (with us) at the limit. It is perhaps fitting too that one of his last texts would return to one of his first—like the infinite refrain of a song.

Tasked with the duty of commenting on a book written over forty years ago, in the new preface to *Ego Sum*, Nancy nevertheless admitted his reluctance to read the work again. How to revisit a philosophical text that had "never ceased reworking, repeating, and renewing itself within me"—a text that seemingly left its traces everywhere in the present?[14] After all, this is the very spirit of *Ego Sum* itself, which presents a singular encounter with the Cartesian legacy, its most radical and exigent moments, and its claim to the foundational logics of contemporary philosophy. Remembering *Ego*

Sum was thus a question of remembering what in Descartes still calls upon the present of our thought, even though nearly half a century has now passed since the problem of the Subject felt urgent: "His name, his portrait, the phrase *cogito ergo sum* cling to the whole of our philosophical memory as a kind of emblem to which only a few are equal" (*Ego Sum*, xi–xii). Nevertheless, it is also in *Ego Sum* that Nancy heard the "whisper" of a different Descartes—a whisper that issued from a mouth yawning at the heart of his philosophy.[15] If indeed *Hymne Stomique* is the proem of *Ego Sum*, it is because *Hymne Stomique* is the proem to the very task of philosophy itself, which is to say, a task that issues not from the cogito (i.e., to pursue truth) but from the "ordeal" of an originary opening—a mouth before philosophy.[16]

Hymne Stomique opens with the parturition of the mouth that is also the engendering of gendered progenitors: "father exhaled, mother absorbed," a mingling that is as surprisingly perverse as it is archaically assumed. For in the next opening lines, these births seem to derive from out of fellatio or cunnilingus: "male sucked up into swarming cloud / female sucked swallowed, / you passage inside and out / from top to bottom and their mixings, / their immixture their mastication." At the same time, the mouth is a "porous space as called for by the order of things" that it at times shores up and at others deconstructs in its oscillating syncopated rhythm: "humid joining / of lips disjointed / meat in *logos*, *mythos* in drooling / salut, you the only true / the only real dialectic!"[17]

In the second song, the mouth, voracious in its "hunger appetite desire / demand wait want / thirst attraction hope," swallows classification and consumes differentiation: "you the mixer the masher / sovereign of amalgamations." Hunger "sharpens its edge" along tooth and jaw, where everything is "consumed curdled clotted crushed," and in its excess and expenditure the mouth is sovereignly unconsummated "through that other mouth"—wherein the inescapable echo of Bataille throughout *Stoma* is first heard. In the third song, we get yet another non-dialectical split in the "twin sisters" *Os* and *Bucca* (oral mouth of logos and prelinguistic mouth of babbling), the daughters of Stoma who, in the infinity of their indiscernible doubling, refuse every form of sublation except the "raising . . . up to biting teeth."

Indeed, "*Bucca* becomes *Os* as same changes into same," and with this opening line of the fourth song the mouth is not simply a figure of but *is* that alteration that Nancy theorized in his "Preamble" to *The Discourse of the Syncope* as "the same."[18] For the mouth's twinning and twofolded doubleness (*os* and *bucca*, lip and lip, inside and outside) is "the sameness of the same produced by the same [the mouth] as its alteration [the mouth's syncopated rhythmic or a-rhythmic breathing, crying, barking, etc.]"[19] If the mouth cries out here, it is because it is always something other than its name. Following Nancy's theoretical exposition, we come to understand that the mouth is one corporeal affirmation of the undecidable, which is to say, the withdrawal from the absolute, the total, the complete. Like the same, the mouth "undecides itself": "it undoes itself as it constitutes itself, fissures itself in the very gesture and instant in which it overcomes, fixes, and effaces its fissures."[20] In other words, in the clinamen of its sheer opening and closing—its dis-enclosure—the mouth is the infinite syncopation of the same, which is to say: chaos. As Nancy goes on to write: "*Chaos* is perhaps the proper name itself, the name of the Same that inscribes its syncope [as a mouth does]—and, as a result, the 'mythological' name that 'logic' failed to diminish."[21]

It is not until the fifth song that we arrive at the birth of the human voice and speech, there, where "a sound . . . is worthy of sense." We understand that what emanates from the mouth need not be true, but nonetheless utterance is one of the "truths" of the mouth to the extent that speaking, and any other form of utterance, "speaks" (and by speaking affirms) opening and naked exposure as the mouth's truth. Thus, enunciation is understood "first and foremost" as "the absence of a meaning" given "the multiplicity of languages each with its meaning to each its secret voice." This plurality exists in each word, an anonymous singularity ("no one's voice addressed to each and all") that in the infinity of its finitude can never be the last word. Instead, each word, in the very secrecy of its ending, is an ending where each "meaning" is elliptical in its sense: "each word can mark an ending / as each time the mouth closes." This secrecy marks—precisely by not marking (or secretly marking)—the absence of definitive closure (when lips touch, one pair or more, are they ever not partly open?). It is for this reason that Nancy writes that meaning (or sense, *sens*) "is swallowed up it dances on the waves / foaming infinitely / its froth its profusion its debauchery its luxuriance / its ever-renewed beginning-again," and thereby alludes to the image with which Hegel ended his *Phenomenology of Spirit* (itself a variation on a phrase by Schiller): "From the chalice of this realm of spirits foams forth for him his own infinitude."[22]

Perhaps it is only appropriate that after the human voice speaks the mouth responds—and not for the last time but again, two more times before the end of the poem. The mouth (it's an ear too!) first responds because it can hear what it is forced to take in: the "loudmouth hilarious clamorings / . . . speeches harangues parables sermons racket chatter" of the human voice. The latter's bestial stupidity mirrors "the pain that tears me [the mouth] apart / not only when you scream / but also when you sing." Why does this tearing and rending of the mouth happen no matter what? Because, as Nancy says, the very opening of the mouth is the pulling apart of its lips and the ripping of their corners; chewing is its own daily torment, and kissing is, for the mouth, not a loving embrace but a cruel smothering. Always-already split, the mouth speaks *of* and from *out* of its fragility, which is at once the source of its indestructibility and the condition for its relentless torture and abuse, its gagging and suffocating— the insistence of putting words into it. It is the mouth that says, "*noli me frangere*" (don't shatter me, don't fragment me).[23]

As the poem unfolds, multilingualism is introduced in the sixth song by the way of the singular plurality of language that makes tongues of every tongue, "each tongue in every other tongue," and therefore also never far from the erotically doubled sameness of *baiser* (to kiss, to fuck). Whitman-esque song, here sung to the joys of song in the seventh, is immediately interrupted by the response of the mouth, which speaks of the silence in every song that it holds, suspends, and thereby preserves, but also by which the mouth is interminably silenced. Hence the mouth's closing plea: "Know that it is hard not having an end." The eighth and ninth songs are devoted, respectively, to liquifying consumption and lyrical recitation, and in the tenth and penultimate song, we are sent along the murky paths deep down into the stomatic depths of the abject and ejected, there, where any recapitulated hope to return to the subject is rejected. As Marie-Eve Morin has recently written: "The withdrawal of the subject, where ego is sustained by nothing, happens 'as soon as I open the mouth.' The mouth, as the place of intimacy, is abyssal. Why? Because it is impossible to say that it belongs to me, that it is mine."[24] Indeed, we can go a bit farther and say that it is not even that the "I" opens the mouth but that the mouth in and as its opening makes the body (open), and in creating this stoma gives birth to an I that is always already exposed, cast out, and expropriated from itself.

Thus, while it has rarely been thought or spoken of in this way, it is perhaps time that we recognize (beyond the merely anatomical) that the mouth is an extremity, meaning, that of the body which is most exterior.[25] The outside is "in" the mouth and this originary intrusion is what makes of the mouth a corporeal opening, a stoma. As Morin explains, just as "Nancy will read *ego sum* as a sort of pure performative, a performative without underlying substrate or subject," so too is the stomatic mouth for Nancy the name for this very absence of foundation or ground.[26] In other words, the subject, ego, or I, does not preexist the mouth's opening, including in the form of enunciation, constative, or performative speech, or even breath, but instead is born from out of this abyss and its rhythmic gaping. Indeed, by the eleventh and last song, which joyously opens: "Stoma, it is you who swallows us! / Stoma, it is you who speaks us!" we arrive at the insight that the mouth makes us, and realize that Nancy's poem has been, all along, a hymn to stoma in praise of and gratitude for what of us is stomatic.

Freedom of speech, gag orders, the freedom not to speak, and the right to remain silent, forced confessions through coercion and torture. Speaking the truth and/or lying. The masking (or unmasking), the veiling (unveiling) of mouths. Mouths that spread and open wide to take in non-human life. The freedom to remain anonymous, and for one's identity and place in the world to be left not entirely tracked. Whom can you kiss, where and how; whisper to or shout at, chant with or pray to? The intimacy of the sleeping mouth: drooling, murmuring, moaning, sighing, gasping, snoring. "I can't breathe," but also the freedom to hold one's breath, or to die of asphyxiation. Hunger, malnutrition, and starvation, but also the ritualized freedom of the one who fasts, and the political freedom of the hunger-striker. Sickness and disease, but the freedom to play too: teeth on flesh, my tongue for yours, the right to love without limit—even to do some violence. The multiplicity of languages (heritage, native, given, appropriated), accents, idioms, and jargons. But also the universalizing of English as global patois, and a pervasiveness infinitely modulated thanks to tone, modulation, cadence, timbre, and other qualities of a mouth's music.[27] It is impossible for us not to think of each of these experiences and expirations of freedom when reading Nancy's *Hymne Stomique*, since each is the provocation of thought—that which forces a critical consideration of the particular ethical or political event but also in the sense of freedom as that which "gives thought to thought."[28] These instances thus speak to both the freedoms most saliently provoked by our present (which is both already receding and arriving newly) but also those freedoms that we undergo constantly.[29] This is especially the case given that in the mouth's third and last response (by which the poem ends), the mouth reverses the hierarchy and reminds us it is the mouth that thinks and that thinks us: "Through me there you are spoken / Through me there you are sung / Through me kissed coupled liquidated." It is not the cogito / ego that thinks, but it is from out of the mouth that we come to think. Before the Cartesian division of *res cogitans* and *res extensa*, there is *res patere* (the open thing). The opening or the closing of the mouth is the birth of *each time*, the singularity of temporality and the temporality of singularity. Which is also, at the same time, the material withdrawal of all substance and the empirical exposure to the Outside, and thus where freedom is at stake, each time, just this once. "Singularity consists in the 'just once, this time,' whose mere enunciation—similar to the infant's cry at birth, and it is necessarily *each time* a question of birth . . . it is each time freedom that is singularly *born*. (And it is birth that *frees*)."[30]

The opening but also the closing of the mouth—that syncopated rhythm—replaces the dialectic, from birth until death, the latter of which, in its last gasp, last breath, is the last birth of singularity. This birth is interminable, and, as Nancy has argued, to the extent that there is interminable beginning, there is freedom. "If freedom gives thought to thought . . . this happens in the materially transcendent experience of a *mouth* at whose opening—neither substance nor figure, a nonplace at the limit of which thought passes into thought—thought tempts chance and takes the risk (*experiri*) of thinking with the inaugural intensity of a cry."[31] With *Hymne Stomique*, Nancy reminds us, once again, that thinking is not only somatic but more precisely *stomatic*, and that stoma is the inauguration of thinking and the patency of existence, each time, just this once.

Bibliography

Armstrong, Philip. "Buccal Exscriptions: Ann Hamilton's *face to face* Photographs." *Parallax* 97, no. 4 (October–December 2020): 366–83. Edited by John Paul Ricco, Stefanie Heine, and Philippe Haensler.

Badiou, Alain, and Jean-Luc Nancy. *German Philosophy: A Dialogue*. Edited and with an afterword by Jan Völker. Translated by Richard Lambert. Cambridge, MA: MIT Press, 2018.

Bataille, Georges. *Theory of Religion*. Translated by Robert Hurley. New York: Zone Books, 1992.

Guyer, Sara. "Buccal Reading." *CR: New Centennial Review* 7, no. 2 (fall 2007): 71–89.

Gyenge, Andrea. "*Fabula, Bucca, Humanitas*: On *Ego Sum*." In *Understanding Nancy, Understanding Modernism*. New York: Bloomsbury, forthcoming.

Kamuf, Peggy. "Béance." *CR: New Centennial Review* 7, no. 2 (fall 2007): 37–56.

LaBelle, Brandon. *Lexicon of the Mouth: Poetics and Politics of Voice and the Oral Imaginary*. New York: Bloomsbury, 2014.

Morin, Marie-Eve. "How Do We Live Here? Abyssal Intimacies in Jean-Luc Nancy's *La Ville au Loin*." *Parrhesia* 25 (2016): 110–28.

Nancy, Jean-Luc. "Beheaded Sun (Soleil cou coupé)." Translated by Bruce Gold and Brian Holmes. *Qui Parle* 3, no. 2 (fall 1989): 41–53.

———. *The Inoperative Community*. Edited by Peter Connor. Minneapolis: University of Minnesota Press, 1991.

———. *The Birth to Presence*. Translated by Brian Holmes et al. Stanford: Stanford University Press, 1993.

———. *The Experience of Freedom*. Translated by Bridget McDonald. Stanford: Stanford University Press, 1993.

———. *Résistance de la poésie*. Bordeaux: William Blake, 1997. English translation available at https://fragilekeys.com/2014/04/26/resistance-of-poetry/.

———. *Corpus*. Translated by Richard A. Rand. New York: Fordham University Press, 2008.

———. *The Discourse of the Syncope: Logodaedalus*. Translated by Saul Anton. Stanford: Stanford University Press, 2008.

———. "Fantastic Phenomena." *Research in Phenomenology* 41 (2011): 228–37.

———. *Adoration: The Deconstruction of Christianity II*. Translated by John McKeane. New York: Fordham University Press, 2013.

———. *Ego Sum: Corpus, Anima, Fabula*. Translated by Marie-Eve Morin. New York: Fordham University Press, 2016.

———. *Expectation: Philosophy, Literature*. Translated by Robert Bononno. New York: Fordham University Press, 2018.

Ricco, John Paul. "Drool: Liquid Fore-Speech of the Fore-Scene." *World Picture* 10 (spring 2015). http://www.worldpicturejournal.com/WP_10/Ricco_10.html.

PART III

Scandalous Death

1

Around people who were close to him, Philippe Lacoue-Labarthe would sometimes cry out with anger: "Death is a scandal! It's intolerable!" When he died almost fourteen years ago, prematurely and after a long illness, he was very calm. He said he did not want any futile and aggressive treatments. Jacques Derrida, for his part, said to me one day when he was already quite ill: "You know, what I would prefer is a good old resurrection." (He was alluding to my attempt to propose a demythologized interpretation of *anastasis*—raising or resurrection.) His humor conveyed both the impossibility of believing in another life and a bitter regret that it be this way. He too died well short of the age that he might have hoped for. Several years before that, Jean-François Lyotard, aware that he was terminally ill, told me with a mischievous smile, "One must resist." I didn't dare ask him what it was necessary to resist—death or the refusal of death. I think he wanted to remain ambiguous. Werner Hamacher, struck down at seventy-one in his prime, had no desire to die but did not want to prolong useless care measures either.

Each of them was philosopher—and not merely "a philosopher"—in the most consummate sense of the word. Their words and attitudes were not foreign or, even less, contrary to their philosophical *ethos* (and this is why I talk about them without any indiscretion: they belong to their thought; I am convinced that many others offer similar testimonies). Each of them testifies—in a way that is vehement or ironic, cold or fierce—to a contrast or even a dissent between the philosopher within them, and the unbearable and always scandalous proximity to death in front of them.

Philosophy is neither an antidote to death—to the heartbreak of the death of the other, to the recoil before one's own death—nor training for some "good death." If "to philosophize is to learn to die," as Montaigne said after Cicero, it is not a question of acquiring a knowledge but rather of recognizing that any knowledge is coupled with an irreducible non-knowledge about death—and about life, for that matter. Such a not knowing is not some kind of ignorance that would be provisional: its "objects" (death, life, as well as love or beauty, or body, and truth) have nothing to do with knowledge. That is, they do not demand to be mastered, or even identified—other than by their surprising, shattering, and disorienting nature.

This is why mourning subsides, in a sense, but never completely. Its pain can fade. It can even seem to disappear: it is always ready to rear its head again, like an almost painless suffering that is nonetheless acute, instantaneous, that boils down to the fact that there is no reason why the other has died [*disparu*].

2

This does not mean that what is wounded is the principle of sufficient reason. It is not a question of principle or reason, and one can have contested such a principle, as has been done for a long time, without actually conceding that death is one of the objects of a not knowing. For these objects—love, beauty, truth, body, or life—in their infinite and surely painful departures as well, do not wound like death does. They leave the trace of a passage, and in this trace we still taste something of them. But the trace left by death is not the trace of its passage but of its disappearance. It is precisely this not knowing that is unbearable.

All of the consolations that memories, testimonies, and tributes can offer—for example, in Proust, Bergotte's books in the illuminated storefront windows of bookshops[1]—do not ever change anything about the bite of definitive absence.

This is why the exemplary philosophical death, the death of Socrates, is, from the point of view of the one who dies, only a way of accessing the true world or the truth of the world, but the one who stages this death—Plato—does not forget to recount the followers' tears. And he himself, Plato, is not there; he is sick (this is why the story is told by Phaedo): it is as if this admirable philosophical accomplishment were at the same time unbearable for him.

In fact, philosophy has never really attempted to diminish or overcome death. On the contrary, it has never ceased to turn away from death all the while looking straight into its dreadful obscurity. Death, indeed—philosophy has inherited its question or its aporia, and one can even say that philosophy came into being with the formation of this question and the aporia that responds to it.

Up until then, and everywhere outside of the world where philosophy took place,[2] death was or still remains a passage to another world of existence or presence. In its Western mutation—marked by a new worry in Egypt about the conditions and outcome of the passage—the passage became an impasse. Instead of being able to communicate in various ways with the dead, we lose them. It is this loss that philosophy must work to compensate for, and it is in this way that one comes to distinguish between a body and a soul or spirit.

This has gone as far as the point where Spinoza conceived of the difference between an eternal part of spirit, situated in God, and a part linked to the duration of mortal life. Or to the point where one refers to death, as Hegel does, as an "inactuality," which does not mean that death does not come but rather that it puts an end to actuality, to the act of an individual's reality. At the same time, the Spirit of the world, like Spinoza's Substance, is the genuine place where actuality persists through death itself.[3]

In psychoanalytic terms, one could say that these philosophers practice denial. In fact, one can imagine a psychoanalysis of philosophy, and it is a small part of what we are doing when we go back to philosophy's infancy. But denial is a complicated thing and it reveals what it denies as well. The appeal to Substance or Spirit entails a recognition of the formidable—abysmal—gap that separates pure loss and the sense of eternity (that is, outside of time) that, according to Spinoza, we "feel and know."[4] What is tasked with filling this gap only intensifies it.

3

This intensification nevertheless also brings out the eternity that Rimbaud found again, not by chance, in 1872.[5]

This outside of time where death resides—and with it beauty, love, and truth—can offer its withdrawal at any moment. In death, this outside leaves the succession of moments definitively. But where there are no references left for it, that is, when Substance or Spirit are themselves dead (or, what amounts to the same thing, reduced to the state of phantasms), then even if the poet finds eternity again—in 1872, for example—he still hears "the deadly hissings and the hoarse music that the world, far behind us, hurls at our mother of beauty."⁶ The world "far behind us" is the world that hurries toward a goal, toward a triumph over time that would succeed in turning the future into a present while relieving itself of the past. This is what is called technoscientific progress.

In this progress, there is no place left for death. Hence, there is no place for its unbearable scandal. One still suffers with each death, but this suffering is the business of individuals, and individuals themselves (who are said to embody true life!) do not count for much compared to the imposing machine of progress and its domination. To each their own mourning, but generally speaking, one bids farewell to mourning: one does not grieve for it; it disappears little by little like the smoke of crematoriums. This smoke is undoubtedly not that of the pyre, which here and there can still offer *passages* to those who perform the ritual. It is an evasion, a sleight of hand [*un tour de passe-passe*]. Beyond the passage and the impasse, one finds the sleight of hand.

During the same time that one murders, tortures, starves, drowns, persecutes, and condemns or excludes by the millions every day, the population of the world grows. Everywhere mothers scream in despair, children in terror, and men in anger. Nowhere can they be heard because listening is no longer possible. We do not understand the songs of mourners anymore, and requiems are only magnificent pieces of music. What happened during the first wave of the coronavirus in Italy (and we can imagine in China, too) with its almost hidden burials and what is happening today in Brazil and in India provide a sort of caricature of our situation: no longer "how to honor the dead" but "how to dispose of them."

More broadly, death—like life if we consider the whole of medical practices and biogenetic projects—is subjected to that which is most contradictory to it: to a chronological succession, the measure of which is given by a constant surpassing of the present, of the pause or stop, of attention or ecstasy (if it is possible to use that word). What persists tends to be nothing more than a continuous beat as the measure of a being. In this way, death becomes the measure of life rather than being its excess.

And of course, this is how we have always watched for, waited for, and taken note of death: by means of the breath, the pulse, the encephalogram. Yet this is how one removes from death its approach, imminence, or occurrence. This has been done in all cultures, but the meaning is different depending on whether it's a matter of a passage, a handing over even, or an impasse.

4

The philosophical twentieth century was traversed by a trajectory that began with "being-towards-death" (Heidegger) and culminated in "life-death" (Derrida)—a trajectory that can also be represented as beginning with Freud's death drive and ending with, as Lacan put it, "the millions of men for whom the pain of existing is the original evidence."[7] What is at stake is the excess of death: how to recognize in its incommensurable character, and hence inevitably its scandalous character, something of the order of a sense and not an absurdity or incongruousness?

Each of the statements just evoked has remained more or less a dead letter—as we must indeed call it—for a variety of reasons: the discredit that Heidegger brought upon his own work, the difficulty of confronting an opposition between two non-dialectical antitheses, and, finally, the dominating, self-satisfied avidity that subjugates entire peoples.

So many ways of not being able or willing to hear. One cannot when one is too subjected to the pressures of an opinion that only worries about death in a private and expeditious way. One is not willing to when one clings to the power of production and invention. Or else one is neither able nor willing to because one has eliminated or diminished the strangeness of death.

Now, this strangeness is the most profound there is. It is what makes us speaking and thinking animals. The philosophical task is not to reduce or dismiss this strangeness. It is not to recognize that death is unfortunate but that one has to deal with it even if it is impossible. This task is really and truly to affirm the scandal of death in order to ask, in the same breath, what such a great and essential scandal, which no condemnation or exclusion can diminish, might mean.

Thinking our scandalous existence and with it that of all living beings. Thinking the scandal of a movement—process or impulse, formation or production—of which an essential character is to exhaust itself. Thinking the scandal that this exhaustion constitutes when it is forbidden to project a kind of hyperlife without death. But in order to do this, it is first necessary to ask how such a scandal is possible.

Philosophy prides itself on beginning with Socrates's death: scandalous with regard to Socrates's virtue and wisdom, as well as his age, this death is transfigured into an entry into truth. One can push the psychoanalysis a bit further: a scandalous death is needed to bring to light philosophical death, that is, the death that redeems the scandal of death in general. Redeems it, compensates for it, justifies it, repairs it, or however one wants to say it—but in the end this comes down to recognizing it.

Philosophy relies on what begins as a denial and culminates in the affirmation of a head-on confrontation with the scandal. At its core, all philosophy is situated between Nietzsche, who affirms that one saves one's personal life from death in living universal life, and Wittgenstein, who declares that death is not an event within life. If one looks closely, this does not at all undermine Christian, Muslim, Buddhist, or Brahmanist beliefs—except that philosophy does not cover up the obscure and dreadful certainty of death, and hence its scandal, with representations. And it is indeed such an uncompromising confrontation that has been proposed all throughout the trajectory of twentieth-century thought.

5

The problem of the twenty-first century in this regard has to do with the fact that, far from attempting to deepen and sharpen this confrontation, it strives to cover it up with a double layer of life and death.

Human life and the life of all living beings are consecrated by the sovereign values of dignity, respectability, and protection at the same time as all forms of killing are multiplied and trivialized—from death camps to firearm possessions, from techno-economic devastation to the closing of borders, from the unbearable conditions of life to the murderous conditions of migration. Never has life been such an empty concept as when it has been adorned with the ribbons of humanism and the flowers of ecology.

Health and medicine testify to this remarkably. The absolute rule of medicine is to sustain human life as much as possible. The more it is possible, then, to prolong life—defined as cerebral activity—the more appropriate it is to do so. As we know, lives sustained indefinitely in a state of mere breathing raises questions about futile and aggressive treatment but also, in the end, about all of the very clever means that are mobilized to render life extendable—from the monitoring of diets to organ transplants and soon other regenerative techniques. From there onward, everything gets muddled easily: the role of the State in the implementation of these techniques raises the specter of a dangerous kind of control, all while one expects the same State to provide for the security of life. The Covid-19 pandemic offers us glaring illustrations of this mess every day, and no politics knows how to sort it out.

Among these characteristic examples, none will have been more striking than the confrontation between advocates of stronger protections for the elderly and advocates of a supposedly egalitarian or communitarian protection that would provide younger people more freedom with regard to work. Philosophers weighed in, from different points of view (provided a point of view can amount to a philosophy).

For some, it was a question of the productivity of the lives in question, with some having become sterile while others were in full force. For others, on the contrary, it was a question of the necessity of refusing all calculation, and hence all distinction and all health care measures. Ideology of production or ideology of abstention: *extremes meet*. Philosophical rigor is not in between the two, nor beyond them. It is of another nature: it lies in the confrontation with death that I have suggested. Looking death in the eye, knowing that one will not see anything, that there is nothing to see. That there is something unbearable there indeed, which is nothing other than what our condition as speaking animals must bear.

Baudelaire invokes Death so

> That we would wander Hell and Heaven through,
> Deep in the Unknown seeking something *new*![8]

If Baudelaire underscores the "new," it is as the ground of the unknown, itself unknowable and *as such* absolutely true. He does not call for a different representation but for a novel way of thinking.

OCTOBER 2020
—*Translated by Marie-Eve Morin and Travis Holloway*

Notes

Introduction

1. [*Cruor* was first published as a separate book, along with "Leçon" and "Nostalgie du père," by Editions Galilée. It was the last work that Nancy completed before his death in 2021.—Trans.] Jean-Luc Nancy, *Corpus* (Paris: Métailié, 1992; reissued in 2002 and 2006). [This text was published in English, along with the original French version and several other essays, in Nancy, *Corpus*, trans. Richard Rand (New York: Fordham University Press, 2008), 2–121.—Trans.]

2. [*Ex-peausition* is a word invented by Nancy playing on *exposition* (exposure) and *peau* (skin). See *Corpus*, 32, 33ff.—Trans.]

3. I am attempting in my own way to respond to the question formulated by Derrida in *Circumfession* (1991)—"What is demanded of us by the crude, the raw?"—as we must hear it proffered by him in the audiobook produced by Éditions de Femmes (rereleased in 2020). The sonority of "*cru*" makes resonate a wound in language, one that we immediately sense as touching on the most intimate, the most sensitive and alive, also the most dead. ["Circumfession," in Geoffrey Bennington and Jacques Derrida, *Jacques Derrida* (Chicago: University of Chicago Press, 1993), 3.]

4. Leonardo da Vinci, *The Notebooks*, ed. Thereza Wells (Oxford: Oxford University Press [Oxford World Classics], 1952/2008), 239. What progress we've made since da Vinci!

5. As Hans Blumenberg showed in the book he published with that title in 1966. [*The Legitimacy of the Modern Age*, trans. Robert M. Wallace (Cambridge, MA: MIT Press, 1983).]

6. It would be impossible to provide a bibliography here. However, we must underscore the importance of the appearance of Freud in the theoretical field, es-

pecially if we link it—as I will suggest later—to a profound movement of thought, initiated by Schopenhauer and even by Rousseau, in which the assurances of the Enlightenment are placed in doubt. The triumphant deployment of technocapitalism and of the bourgeoisie was accompanied by an anxiety and a suspicion which Baudelaire, and later Benjamin (also Rimbaud), thought in terms of the possibility that this triumph may be a comedy.

7. [*Des corps, ça se touche*: this phrase exemplifies some of the difficulties this translation has had to grapple with and that are worth pointing out briefly here. *Des corps*: bodies; *ça se touche*: literally, it (this thing we call bodies) touches itself, is touched, and, as a plurality also implied by the indefinite *ça*, they touch each other. The reflexive verb *se toucher* says all of this at once. Nancy continually plays on the polysemy of reflexive verbal constructions in French. I have tried to render these senses throughout as elegantly and as fully as possible, at times through hendiadys, at times by placing the reflexive object (*each other, itself*) at the end of a series of verbs instead of throughout, and at times by playing on the register of the middle voice in English—so that a phrase such as "bodies touch" can blur active and passive while also evoking, albeit less literally, an implicit reciprocity. Finally, the *ça*, the *it*, makes a first (untranslatable) appearance here, in a phrasing that plays on colloquial speech while also leading us toward the enlarged sense of a Freudian *id* (*le ça* in French) that will be at issue in later sections. I have at times marked the use of *ça* with an italicized *it* to highlight Nancy's deliberate and frequent recourse to it (sometimes italicized by him), which otherwise would stand out less clearly in English (whereas in French it is more distinct and would often be translated as a more emphatic *that* or *this*, as it is on occasion here), and so to distinguish it from other third-person pronouns in French.—Trans.]

Cruor

1. Julio Cortázar, *From the Observatory*, trans. Anne McLean (Brooklyn, NY: Archipelago Books, 2011), 13.

2. [*Pulsion*: I introduce here a clarification that Nancy mentions below in section 2, namely that the French word for drive, in Freudian and other senses, evokes more clearly the pulse and pulsation that will be crucial for the reflections developed here.—Trans.]

3. [*Poussé à battre*: literally "pushed to beat." The verb *pousser*, like the English *push*, is also related etymologically to pulse, etc. It occurs often in this text, as does the noun form *poussée*, a push, press, thrust, impulse, or drive. *Pousser* can also mean "to grow," especially for plants or body parts (hair, nails, teeth, wings). Likewise *repousser* can mean repulse, push away, or push back (including in the sense of postpone, defer), or even push or pulse again (re-pulse), a sense on which Nancy plays at times. Where possible I have opted to translate these terms with *push* and related forms to keep this resonance clear, while also occasionally using *press* and variations or, as here, the passive *driven*.—Trans.]

4. On the subject of the "self" and the "ego," it is certain that a passage through the thought of Melanie Klein would be profitable. But I do not have the means to do this.

5. Disputes can arise, identities are already rivals. It is rare, however, that the mother does not put things in order. The mother's preference for one or the other implies the nomination of each one. (We would thus touch on the maternal preference from which proceeds for Freud the awakening of the first poet; we will return to this.)

6. [*Ça pulse, donc ça s'écarte.* Nancy's French sentence more clearly echoes (and term for term radically revises) the famous statement by Descartes: *Je pense, donc je suis*, I think, therefore I am—and even ends on a rhyme with the philosopher's name.—Trans.]

7. *Mimesis* without model: this is the major axis of Lacoue-Labarthe's thought. Let us add this as well: *similis* in Latin comes from the root *sem*, "once," to which corresponds also the Greek *homos* (equivalent of *similis*). "Once" is distinguished from the unique and exclusive "one" (the root of which is *hèn* or *oin*). Once—one time—necessarily implies other times. In all rigor, there can be no "only once." Nor an only self.

8. [Note that the French expression "ça ne ressemble à rien," literally "it resembles nothing," tends to be rather a putdown compared to the more complimentary-sounding English expression used here.—Trans.]

9. [In French (unlike in English, where this meaning has become outmoded) *instance* maintains a sense of *insistence*—the register of instigation, incitement, or pressing urgency that is of most interest to Nancy here—and often indicates an "instance of authority," the seat or institutional embodiment of an official authoritative function, such as a court of law. It does not mean as in English a particular case or example, although in a way Nancy will link it here to this aspect through the temporality of "une fois," that is, time in the sense of a "one time, once . . ." inextricable from its others.—Trans.]

10. See chapter VII of *The Interpretation of Dreams*. It should be noted that in German the word *instantia* underwent the same evolution as in French.

11. Philippe Lacoue-Labarthe, *Phrase*, "Phrase XVII," trans. Leslie Hill (Albany: State University of New York Press, 2018), 72. ["Desistance" is the title of an essay on Lacoue-Labarthe by Jacques Derrida, published in English as an introduction to Lacoue-Labarthe, *Typography: Mimesis, Philosophy, Politics*, trans. Christopher Fynsk (Stanford: Stanford University Press, 1998), 1–42.—Trans.]

12. Jacques Nouet, *L'Homme d'oraison*, 1684 ("a glorious body would shine on the world more light than the sun"). The theology of the glorious body is a way to confer on the body—on the distinct, on the finite—an absolute plenitude of sense.

13. The prehistory of the Christian eucharist would be long and in part still remains to be done. It would have to consider the relation of bread to the nourishing earth, and of wine to drunkenness, and therefore to two divine orders (Ceres

and Dionysos), but also the common process of fermentation, as well as the combination of solid and liquid.

14. Fernando Pessoa, *Faust* (Paris: Christian Bourgois, 1990), 155.

15. [*Se présentant, s'observant, s'approchant et s'éloignant. Se considérant et se saluant.* . . . It is worth noting again some of the implications for Nancy's thought contained in his language, which are more difficult to convey as fully and elegantly in English. While his stated emphasis here is on reciprocity, this series of indefinite reflexive verbs maintains the ambiguity—or rather the sense of an inclusive and simultaneous set of distinct but enmeshed and interdependent relations—between singular self-reflexive actions (e.g., observing oneself), dual reciprocities (two bodies observing one another), and multiple open-ended intermingling (a number of bodies observing themselves, others, and each other, multiply and singly, all at once).—Trans.]

16. Werner Hamacher, *Pleroma* (Paris: Galilee, 1996), 283; Jacques Derrida, *Glas* (Paris: Galilee, 1974), 46. ["(Me) faire chier" in French means literally "to make [me] shit" but is used most often to say "you're extremely annoying" or "a pain in the ass" (*tu me fais chier*). Nancy, by way of Hamacher and Derrida, is playing on both registers here. See also Nancy's note on this point below.—Trans.]

17. Why does the scatological lexicon take on so many negative values of the unbearable, or even the inadmissible? Because it's a question of waste, even though the evacuation of this waste is a deliverance. It is only for the other that my shit is offensive. Likewise "*conchier*" has the exclusive sense of "soiling with excrement." The expression "faire chier," meaning "annoy, anger, exasperate," implies that the evacuation is painful to me. Perhaps precisely the genius of the language here is that it thinks together the alternative and the co-belonging of self and other. Similar remarks can be made regarding the sexual lexicon (*Fuck you!*). [This parenthetical remark is in English in the original.—Trans.]

18. [*Work* here translates *oeuvrer*.—Trans.]

19. And this applies also when procreation is avoided or is impossible: the sexual relation is in itself a glory, a brilliance, an *éclat*, a bedazzlement. The child, when a child comes, is the same glory set free from the relation and ready for other instances of brilliance.

20. Nietzsche, *Zarathustra*, part I, "On the Despisers of the Body," the fourth of "Zarathustra's Speeches." This belongs among the book's fundamental declarations. In these pages, Nietzsche refers to the *Selbst* at times as *er* (masculin) but most often as *es* (neuter).

21. Freud, *The Ego and the Id*, chap. 2; this explanation is taken up again in lecture 31 of the *New Introductory Lectures on Psycho-Analysis*. [In German as in French, the term for "the Id" is simply "the It": *das Es, le Ça*.—Trans.]

22. One can find a very similar usage in a posthumous fragment which (unless I'm mistaken) is not included in *The Will to Power* and was therefore not known to Groddeck or to Freud. Moreover, Nietzsche there distinguishes the Ego from "the entire domain of a 'You' or 'It'"—which remains distant from Freud. Finally, in his *Book of the It*, Groddeck does not mention Nietzsche.

23. We can point out that in German *Selbst* and *Es* (like *self* and *it* in English) are phonetically even more distinct than *soi* and *ça* in French. This is what makes one attentive in this passage from Nietzsche to the frequency of the *es*, used simply to avoid excessive repetition of *Selbst*. I thus allow myself this recourse to the unconscious or to the preconscious of Groddeck and/or of Freud. In this context it is after all only a very small step to make.

24. Nietzsche, *Beyond Good and Evil*, sections 16 and 17.

25. The correspondence between Groddeck and Freud allows us to follow the passage of the *Es* from the former to the latter, as Freud lays out his first sketch of the second topic in a letter to Groddeck (17 April 1921). Later (Christmas 1922), he writes to him: "I think that you have taken the Id from Nietzsche (in a literal, not associative manner)." The formula in parentheses signifies that Groddeck has borrowed a particular term and not the context in which it is thought—which raises curious questions, for it is not necessarily as simple as Freud seems to say.

26. A suggestion I owe to Hélène.

27. Schopenhauer, *The World as Will and Representation*, Second Book, sect. 20.

28. Ibid., sect. 23.

29. Ibid., among others in sect. 27 (translated there as "instinct" as was often done before Freud introduced his concept). [The German word *Trieb* has often been rendered as "instinct" in English translations of Freud, including in the *Standard Edition* of Freud's works. It was partly by way of the French *pulsion*, appearing in Lacan's work, for example (and often used here by Nancy), that it became more common to translate Freud's use of the term into English as *drive*.—Trans.]

30. I can only indicate in passing that it is perfectly possible to show that already in Kant the thing in itself can be understood as dynamic or even pulsive, subject to drives. A drive pushes reason toward the unconditioned: doesn't this drive itself form the unconditioned of reason?

31. Pessoa, *Faust*, 215.

32. Jean-Christophe Bailly, *Poursuites* (Paris: Christian Bourgois, 2003), 55. Allow me to refer as well to my essay *Listening*, trans. Charlotte Mandel (New York: Fordham University Press, 2007).

33. *Selbst* resembles a superlative and Grimm considers it as such: but modern lexicology sees it as a deformation of an older genitive of *selbe* (same). "Of the same," then, which would imply a kind of reflexivity.

34. This Latin form allows us moreover to clearly distinguish *ego* as a "shifter" of the statement and an *egomet* of which I speak ("it was to me myself that this happened . . ."): self separating from self in order to distinctly indicate itself. Alteration and extension combined.

35. Freud, "Findings, Ideas, Problems," SE 23, 300.

36. Ibid. [The *Standard Edition* reads "space" here, but Freud indeed writes spatiality, *Räumlichkeit*.—Trans.]

37. [The three words italicized here are in English in the original.—Trans.]

38. It must be noted that the duality in Hölderlin of the organism and the aorgic, as well as of the role it plays in his thought of the tragic, would need to

be examined, both as one link in the chain leading to Freud and in a comparison of the two relations to the tragic—which, by also including Nietzsche, Benjamin, and Lacoue-Labarthe, as well as Lacan and Gianni Carchia, would constitute a considerable program. I content myself with noting that the tragic is on the horizon of everything I am trying to clarify here.

39. Would there be a connection to make with "the Thing" in Lacan? It's not impossible. The Latin *res*, the *causa*—the matter in question, what acts on and agitates us—and the "anything whatever," the indeterminacy of what is simply there without reason, the "thingy" or "whatever-it-is": something whose origin one finds suspicious. And what origin would not be suspicious?

40. The *différance* found by Derrida can be stated thus: the irreducible alterity of the same.

41. "Mystik: die dunkle Selbstwahrnehmung des Reiches ausserhalb des Ichs, des Es." This note is dated 22 August 1938 (SE 23, 300).

42. "Mysticism" is a term that appears in interesting exchanges in the correspondence between Freud and Groddeck. The former declares that he cannot do without a certain "mysticism." The latter neither approves nor disapproves of it. He finds in it no obstacle to their mutual understanding (see Freud's letter of 12 February 1922). But if the posthumous note is directed at Groddeck, it is difficult to see what "self-perception" could be at issue for him. Freud nonetheless writes to Groddeck: "I naturally do not recognize in your Id my civilized bourgeois Id, denuded of mysticism. Yet you should know that mine derives from yours" (18 June 1925). And one can ask about the precise import here of the word "denuded [*dérobé*]" (in German *berauben* signifies "to steal" and even "to rob" or "ransack [*dévaliser*]" or "to strip or despoil [*dépouiller*]"). At the end of the first chapter of *Civilization and Its Discontents* Freud evokes the possibility that "mysticism" arises in the last instance from the persistence of very ancient physiological elements.

43. Freud, *Analysis Terminable and Interminable*, sect. VI, SE 23, 245.

44. Freud, *Group Psychology and the Analysis of the Ego*, chap. 8, SE 18, 115. [The *Standard Edition* sidesteps the term's connotations by giving "mysterious"; but Freud wrote *mystisch*, which means "mystical."—Trans.]

45. Thanos Zartaloudis, *The Birth of Nomos* (Edinburgh: Edinburgh University Press, 2020), brings together the essential on this subject.

46. Eating the flesh of the other participates therefore in sacrifice. It is not by chance that this becomes a problem for a certain current awareness of cruelty. It is not possible to address this question here. We know that eating the flesh of the other can be related to Eros: biting is not far from kissing, not to mention the lover's cannibalism whose myth Claire Denis, for example, has recounted in her film *Trouble Every Day* (2011).

47. As I write (in June 2020), taking a knee has become a symbolic gesture in the revolt following the murder of George Floyd, a black American who was pinned to the ground by a policeman pressing a knee into his neck.

48. Antonin Artaud, *Oeuvres*, ed. Evelyne Grossman (Paris: Gallimard, 2004 [Quarto edition]), 1385.

49. Georges Bataille, *L'expérience intérieure*, in *Oeuvres complètes* V (Paris: Gallimard, 1973), 88.

50. Karl Marx, *Capital*, vol. 1, chap. 31, trans. Ben Fowkes (New York: Vintage, 1977), 926.

51. Ibid., 923. [The ellipses without brackets are in the quoted text as it appears in the English translation; Nancy's quotation in turn omits phrases, which I have indicated here by ellipses within brackets.—Trans.]

52. Alain Supiot, *Le travail n'est pas une marchandise* (Paris: Collège de France, 2019).

53. Which connects to the thought that the love of the neighbor may be the most dreadful commandment, which would expose one to the cruel enjoyment of the other (in both senses of the genetive). Bernard Baas has presented this very well in "From the Commandement of Love to Inhuman War," published in German in *Sigmund Freud—immer noch Unbehagen in der Kultur* (Berlin/Zurich: Diaphanes, 2009).

54. This is not the case for its English cousin *self* which, however, also previously had this sense.

55. [*L'obscure perception de soi du ça.* This sentence has more of a stutter in French.—Trans.]

56. See Carolin Meister and Jean-Luc Nancy, *Begegnung-Rencontre* (Berlin/Zurich: Diaphanes, 2020).

57. Jacques Derrida, *Etats d'âme de la psychanalyse* (Paris: Galilée, 2000), 12.

58. [These three words (*and, is, have*) are homophones in French: *et, est, ai*.—Trans.]

59. We would have to read the precise analysis of this text by Philippe Choulet in *La Représentation* (Neuilly-sur-Seine: Atlande, 2020), 128ff.

60. Paul Celan, "Die Silbe Schmerz," *Die Niemandsrose*, 1963. [Nancy notes that he translated these lines from the poem himself. The translation given here is from "The Syllable Pain" in Paul Celan, *Selections*, trans. Pierre Joris (Berkeley: University of California Press, 2005), 91, and is very slightly modified to reflect Nancy's rendering.—Trans.]

61. [This very literal translation is adapted from that of William Aggeler.—Trans.]

62. Benjamin Fondane provided an entire analysis of the cruelty engendered by boredom in Baudelaire (*Baudelaire et l'expérience du gouffre* [Paris: Seghers, 1947]).

63. Comte de Lautréamont, *Les Chants de Maldoror*, "Chant deuxième" (1869).

64. Antonin Artaud, *The Theater and Its Double*, trans. Mary Caroline Richards (New York: Grove Weidenfeld, 1958), 99.

65. Michel Houellebecq, *The Possibility of an Island*, trans. Gavin Bowd (New York: Random House, 2006), 42 [translation modified; italics in original].

66. See *On the Parts of Animals*, 673b. Aristotle also refers to accounts saying that in war certain wounds cause laughter, for purely physiological reasons. This indicates the extent to which combat for him is distant from cruelty.—Here as elsewhere, we would need to look more closely at what the Greeks considered valor in war, and at Rome with the cruel spectacles set up in the circus as com-

pletely desacralized sacrifices. Seneca himself criticizes this when he speaks of "human eyes watching human blood flow" (*hominum oculi ab humano cruore*; in the *Moral Letters to Lucilius*, VII).

67. Lacan declared that Freud was "horrified" by this commandment, which Bernard Baas analyzes in terms of the destructive perspective of a universal and unlimited love that could only deliver the other over to my enjoyment "with its entire dimension of horror and cruelty" (paper presented at the international colloquium "La déshumanisation," organized by the Fedepsy [Fédération Européenne de Psychanalyse] in Strasbourg, 12 December 2008). No doubt correct regarding Lacan, if not Freud, this interpretation perhaps shows at the same time that the "love" in question should be understood otherwise than as a desire to enjoy an "object." It is no doubt a question only of the possibility or the impossibility of this other understanding in the entire debate around the Christian commandment.

68. Which preceded Christianity, according to Freud, without specifying further. I cannot comment here on this very interesting remark. In any case, it must be understood that this anteriority is not considerable in time and that nonetheless it draws toward more obscure beginnings what we are in the habit of seeing as a sudden irruption. In other words: the turning point of the West came from a depth that we do not suspect. That is also why it is now going toward unforeseeable abysses.

69. [I have been unable to find this phrase in *Moses and Monotheism*, or in the French translation cited by Nancy: *Moïse et le monothéisme*, trans. A. Berman (Gallimard, 1948), 181.—Trans.]

70. Notably beginning with Anders Nygren's *Agape and Eros*, which first appeared in 1930. Freud does not seem to have read it. In any case, it would be necessary to follow here all the intersecting interests shown during this period for the ways in which affectivity, erotics, the emotions play into various forms of relation and socialization: Scheler and his successors, Buber, Binswanger, Elias, Heidegger, Bataille—which is of course not independent of the context.

71. There would be much to comment on in remarks like the one on the role of incest in cosmologies (in *The Question of Lay Analysis*), on the audacious cosmology of Empedocles ("Analysis Terminable and Interminable") in which he recognizes the prefiguration of the duality of drives (see also above on the "mysticism" of that same philosopher), or on the notions of microcosm and macrocosm (in *Civilization and Its Discontents*).

72. Which of course must not be forgotten: it is a question of the love of God for his creatures, which is neither a desire nor a devourment, but a giving-rise-to-being.

73. One can say that what the Greek world had attempted as *politics* (at the heart of which there was *philia*, conjunction and transmutation of *eros* and *cosmos*), and that had dissolved beginning with Athenian imperialism, was sought again as a *cosmics*—from the "creation of the world" to the "dignity of all."

74. We might even speak of "cherishment": the act that grants a price, the much abused "charity" by which *agape* has been translated.

75. Money according to Marx.

76. Freud, *Three Essays on the Theory of Sexuality*, I, 1, a (SE 7, 148). [This quotation from Freud and those that follow have been slightly modified to reflect Nancy's language.—Trans.]

77. Freud, *Totem and Taboo*, II, 3 (a), "The Treatment of Enemies" (SE 13, 36).

78. From a posthumous fragment. [See Friedrich Hölderlin, *Hymns and Fragments*, trans. Richard Sieburth (Princeton: Princeton University Press, 1984), 222–23. I am translating the French *intime* literally, but *Innig* is often translated as "inward." Likewise for Augustine's *interior intimo meo*: "more inward than the most inward . . ." In Latin *intimo* is a superlative based on the comparative *interior*.—Trans.]

79. Virginia Woolf, *Moments of Being* (New York: Harcourt Brace Jovanovich, 1985), 72.

80. Hermann Broch, *Le Tentateur*, trans. A. Kohn (Paris: Gallimard, 1960), 74.

81. Aurélien Barrau, "Monde," *Météorites* (Paris: Michel Lafon, 2020), 85.

82. Valérie Jouve, *Corps en résistance* (Paris: Filigranes/Jeu de Paume, 2015).

83. Rodolphe Burger, *Environs* (Dernière Bande, 2020).

84. The title of the seminar by Jacques Derrida. [Derrida, *Life Death*, ed. Pascale-Anne Brault and Peggy Kamuf, trans. Pascale-Anne Brault and Michael Naas (Chicago: University of Chicago Press, 2020).]

85. Pierre-Henri Castel, *Le mal qui vient* (Paris: Cerf, 2018), 95.

86. Michel Deguy, *L'Énergie du désespoir, ou d'une poétique continuée par tous les moyens* (Paris: PUF, 1998), 32.

Longing for the Father

The following is a separate essay, initially independent (it was a paper presented at the conference or webinar *Massenpsychologie* organized by several organizations, under the direction of Sergio Benvenuto, in April–May 2021) but whose close links with the preceding will be apparent. The English translation was originally published in the *European Journal of Psychoanalysis*: https://www.journal-psychoanalysis.eu/.

1. For the term *Vatersehnsucht*, see *The Ego and the Id*, III. I will simply indicate the sections in Freud's texts, since I prefer to translate them myself; this will also be useful to those who want to consult the original German or the translations. In this sense the present essay is not a work of erudition.

2. Or around a "supplement," to use Derrida's term.

3. I developed this concept with Philippe Lacoue-Labarthe in *La Panique politique* in 1979 (re-edited by Christian Bourgois in 2013). In English under the same title in *Retreating the Political*, ed. Simon Sparks (New York: Routledge, 1997), 1–28.

4. In 1921, this word *group* [masse] did not have the connotations it does today—either pejorative or revolutionary. It designates the number, the multitude,

the collectivity or the common people, considered for approximately the past fifty years to constitute a group, gathering, or crowd—that is, something problematic when speaking from the individual perspective, as Freud and many others do, except Marxists, for whom the notion of class changes the entire perspective.—The use of the plural for this word in Freud's title corresponds to the plural of Le Bon's "crowds" in the title of his book, on which Freud comments. Because this word is much more widely applied today than in 1900 ("the metro is crowded"), I prefer using the word "group."

5. During his visit to the United States in 1909, Freud expressed the desire to see a wild porcupine.

6. I analyzed this question in *Cruor*, section 8.

7. *The Ego and the Id*, chap. II.

8. As Freud explains in complex and somewhat awkward terms, because he seems to be both discussing the origin and retracing a first prehistoric phase that led from an initial totemic society which gave up the inheritance from the father to a "new family" with multiple fathers who do not have the omnipotence of the original father and are therefore inadequate (which resembles the society contemporaneous with the very first known myths and with the poetry Freud evokes in that section). As a result, the scene is both primary and secondary—which explains the impossibility of identifying a concrete origin.

9. Freud, *Group Psychology II*.

10. Hanns Sachs, *Gemeinsame Tagträume* ("Daydreams in Common"), in *The Creative Unconscious* (Cambridge, MA: Sci-Art Publishers, 1951).

11. Or "archeophilic," as we said in *La Panique politique*.

12. Seminar 1961–1962 on identification, session November 22, 1962.

13. "Every other is an altogether other."

14. In the same seminar.

15. Of course, we should raise the question of the extent of the poet's power, but that will be the subject of another discussion.

16. *Umdeutung* (reinterpretation) can be understood as implying a turn-around (*um-*) or reversal, an inversion, or even a perversion.

17. "A Special Type of Choice of Object Made by Men" (in *Contributions to the Psychology of Love*), 1910 (SE 11, 165). As we know, Freud often commented on the special abilities of poets and artists in general to understand the psyche. In *The Future of an Illusion,* he wrote: "The creation of art heightens feelings of identification, of which every cultural unit stands in so much need" (SE 21, 14).

18. Jacques Lacan, *Œuvres graphiques et manuscrites*, auction catalog (Paris: Hôtel Dassault, 2006).

19. Esther Tellermann, *Freud-Lacan*, "Consultation-document" (Freud-lacan.com). This modern refusal of "poetry-'pouasie'" constitutes a major symptom of the disappearance of myth and of the accompanying nostalgia that had their roots in German romanticism. Nostalgia replaced the father with myth, and this reinforced nostalgia suffers from its inability to bring about a new and originary discourse.

20. Esther Tellermann, *S'apparenter à un poète* (http://www.gnipl.fr/PDF%20insu/Esther%20TELLERMANN%20%20S%E2%80%99apparenter%20%C3%A0%20un%20po%C3%A8te.pdf). The term *apparenter* (to be akin) is taken from Lacan and contrasts with *plate-parenté* (plain kinship): this is the concept on which Tellermann comments.

21. This refers, of course, to Heidegger's *Geworfenheit*—thrown existence.

22. Gilbert Simondon, *Individuation in Light of Notions of Form and Information* (Minneapolis: University of Minnesota Press, 2020). It would be worthwhile to follow closely these analyses made by Simondon, especially in their loose relations with psychoanalysis.

23. This sentence is quoted after a reference to *Group Psychology*. Article: "Logical Time and the Assertion of Anticipated Certainty," *Newsletter of the Freudian Field* 2, no. 2 (fall 1988): 4–22.

24. Study of *milieux*, of environments, therefore of connections, relationships, and exchanges.

25. *The Ego and the Id*, II. The "cap of hearing" appears in the famous drawing in Freud's second topography. Paul Celan took up and transformed the *Hörkappe* to *Hörklappe* (acoustic valve) in his poem *Schief*. See commentary by Jean Bollack: "Celan lit Freud" (Celan reads Freud), *Savoirs et clinique* 1, no. 6 (2005). Celan's poem deserves further interpretation: in short, I would say that it indicates that the poet hears differently, or better, than the analyst.

26. Seminar on identification, May 1962.

27. Lacan's thought cannot be reduced to this Lacanian vulgate. For instance, we might read "L'erre de la métaphore" by Eric Porge, *Essaim*, no. 21 (2008), or his *Voix de l'écho* (Toulouse: Erès, 2012). What displaces the opposition between literal and figurative, from which the idea of metaphor originates, is a subject that would require reading Derrida's "White Mythology" and the discussion with Ricoeur that followed this text. In parallel with this philosophical work, Lacan's writing tended toward a topology. As for me, I would like to return to poetry, that is, to show that if it must become a question of the poem here, it is also necessary to exceed every discourse of knowledge. Not to say more or better, but to give language over to the dimension of saying.

28. Jean-Jacques Rousseau, "Essay on the Origin of Languages," in *The First and Second Discourses and Essay on the Origin of Languages*, trans. Victor Gourevitch (New York: Harper, 1986), 245.

29. On the subject of the voice between psychoanalysis and philosophy, I refer the reader to Bernard Baas, *La voix déliée, L'écho de l'immémorial*, and—forthcoming—*Jouissances de la voix* (which discusses the "embodied voice").

30. This brings to mind Alain Didier-Weil's "appeal to intuition," which was taken up by Lacan.

31. Jean-Christophe Bailly, *Naissance de la phrase* (Nous, 2020), 61.

32. Jacques Derrida, "Qual Quelle: Valéry's Sources," in *Margins of Philosophy*, trans. Alan Bass (Chicago: University of Chicago Press, 1984), 286. It must be made clear that this "immediacy" is only apparent ("seems," Derrida writes). The

voice articulates and therefore is mediated. There is no rigid division between voice and discourse, between sense and signification. Instead, each refers to the other, resonates in the other (which is what makes a "subject"). The question of resonance is also discussed in my book *Listening*, trans. Charlotte Mandel (New York: Fordham University Press, 2007).

33. Kant, *Religion within the Limits of Reason Alone*, I.

34. The passage from the totemic voice to belief and the fact that the sentence quoted from Kant goes on to speak of the "religion of priests" are subjects for a separate discussion.

35. Even to those who don't hear it. As long as the myth is articulated, it touches all the members of the group, it brings about identification. When it no longer does this, and "the myth" becomes propaganda, be it that of a dictator or that of a publicity industry (which is the same thing), the entire group hears, but what it hears is not its voice. Or it ceases precisely thereby to be a group and constitutes itself into a mass, as the word is used today. Bernard Baas examines this question in the chapter "Des clameurs du peuple" in *Jouissances de la voix*.

36. "Aide-mémoire" (1985), in *Comme ci Comme ça* (Paris: Gallimard, 2012), 105.

Stoma

1. [In the original French, the object of this series of apostrophes, "You, the . . ." is marked grammatically by the feminine (*toi la brouilleuse, la mêleuse, la parleuse, etc.* . . .), ostensibly designating throughout the text a series of addresses to the mouth, *la bouche*.—Trans.]

2. [NB: "*cuisson et coction*" have been elided into "stove" and "stone," not least to preserve the tercet form of stanza as well as the alliterative play of plosives in the original.—Trans.]

3. [Nancy uses two striking decasyllabic lines here—a meter especially associated with song and Renaissance lyric poetry in French.—Trans.]

4. [The reference is to George Bataille's "La Bouche" entry in the "Critical Dictionary" (*Documents*). See *Visions of Excess: Selected Writings: 1927–1939*, ed. Allan Stoekl, trans. Allan Stoekl with Carl R. Lovitt and Donald M. Leslie Jr. (Minneapolis: University of Minnesota Press, 1985), 50. See also *Undercover Surrealism: Georges Bataille and Documents*, ed. Dawn Ades and Simon Baker (Cambridge, MA: MIT Press, 2006), 91–92.—Trans.]

5. [Nancy's intertextual reference here is to Mallarmé's celebrated line from *Crise de vers*: "Les langues imparfaites en cela que plusieurs, manque la suprême."—Trans.]

6. [*L'inouï*. The nominal form perhaps rings unusual in English but not in French, where it is synonymous with "the extraordinary." Nancy seems to be playing, however, on the relation and negation of sound/hearing—*in/ouïe*, which the noun invariably also carries in French.—Trans.]

7. [The allusion here is to fragment 206 from Pascal's *Pensées*, "Le silence éternel de ces espaces infinis m'effraie."—Trans.]

8. [*Claquée*, both "exhausted" as *supra* but also the clicking sound one can make with the tongue.—Trans.]

9. [Nancy is likely referencing Psalm 81:10: "I am the Lord your God, who brought you out of the land of Egypt; Open thy mouth wide, and I will fill it."—Trans.]

10. [Nancy is referencing a line from Paul Valéry's "Bouche" text, in *Poems in the Rough*, vol. 2, trans. David Paul (Princeton: Princeton University Press, 2015), 50.—Trans.]

11. [This tercet is in English in the original.—Trans.]

12. ["The poet does not imitate nature: it is well and true that nature speaks in and through his/her mouth." Giacomo Leopardi, *Pensieri: Varia filosofia e di bella leteratura*, vol. 7 (Firenze: Sucessori Le Monnier, 1900), 4372.—Trans.]

13. [Virgil, *Aeneid*, book 1, l. 685: "When [Dido] embraces you, and plants sweet kisses on you,/you'll breathe hidden fire into her, deceive her with your poison."—Trans.]

14. [Paul Celan, *Mirror*, "In the mirror it's Sunday,/in the dream there will be sleeping,/the mouth speaks the truth."—Trans.]

15. [Nancy is citing a ghazal here—a short-form lyric from the Arabo-Persian tradition—translated in 1925 by Marguerite Ferté under the title "Telle qu'il s'en rencontre" ("Woman such as one meets . . ."). Anonymous, *Ghazels* (Paris: Boissard, 1925).—Trans.]

16. [Victor Hugo, "Oh! de mon ardente fièvre" [Oh! in my burning fever], posthumously published, *Dernières oeuvres* [1902].—Trans.]

17. [Nancy is playing on two meanings of *palais* in French: palace and palate [as in the mouth].—Trans.]

Afterword to *Stoma*

1. We would like to thank Philip Armstrong for reading a draft of this afterword, Robert St. Clair for the translation, and Mahité Breton for her advice and assistance on the translation.

2. As cited by Nancy in "Reason Demands Poetry: An Interview with Emmanuel Laugier," in Nancy, *Expectation*, 118. Throughout his career, Nancy wrote on poetry, including the work of Rimbaud, Valéry, Hölderlin, and others. Along with the essays and poems collected in *Expectation*, which includes Nancy's poem from 2014, "Let him kiss me with his mouth's kisses," we wish to highlight Nancy, *Résistance de la poésie*.

3. Nancy, *Expectation*, 122.

4. Bataille, *Theory of Religion*, 22. Nancy cites this phrase many times in his work including in "We Need . . . ," in *Birth to Presence*, 308, as well as in the interview "Reason Demands Poetry," 109.

5. Nancy, "Reason Demands Poetry," 117.

6. Ibid., 112.

7. Nancy, *Adoration*, 20.

8. Or more precisely, as in the first song: "meat in *logos*, *mythos* in drooling."

9. For more on "the buccal" in Nancy's work, see Guyer, "Buccal Reading"; Gyenge, "*Fabula, Bucca, Humanitas*"; Kamuf, "Béance"; and Armstrong, "Buccal Exscriptions."

10. Nancy, "Beheaded Sun," 45.

11. Nancy, *The Inoperative Community*, 30; Nancy, *Experience*, 78.

12. Nancy, "Fantastic Phenomena," 235.

13. Nancy, *Ego Sum*, x.

14. Ibid.

15. Ibid., 12. In the first volume of what is now, with the publication of *Corpus III*, a philosophical trilogy on the body, Nancy spent many of its pages at the threshold points of the body, and where he called for a corpus in honor of corpus: "we'd need a corpus: a catalogue instead of a logos, the enumeration of an empirical logos, without transcendental reasons, a list of gleanings, in random order and completeness, an ongoing stammer of bits and pieces . . . vague in its ordering, always extendable . . ." (*Corpus*, 53, last ellipsis in the original) and a bit further: "We need a corpus of entries into the body: language entries, encyclopedia entries, all the body's introductory topoi. . . . A corpus would be the registration of this long discontinuity of entries (or exits: the door always swings both ways). . . . A body is the topic of its access, its every here/there, its fort/da, its coming-and-going" (*Corpus*, 55). For one impressive attempt to create such a lexicon, see LaBelle, *Lexicon of the Mouth*.

16. Nancy, *Ego Sum*, 112.

17. For an engagement with Nancy's thinking on sleeping and the exorbitant excess of the self/mouth, see Ricco, "Drool."

18. Nancy, *Syncope*, 1–16.

19. Ibid., 9.

20. Ibid., 9, 10.

21. Ibid., 12.

22. In the context of a published dialogue on "German Philosophy" with Alain Badiou, and specifically regarding the question of Hegel's "system," Nancy says, "For me, by contrast, Hegel is equally, not exactly the antisystem, but—I'm not sure what to call it—the hypersystem? The hypersystem that does not cease to systematize itself. As soon as one starts to speak of Hegel, what inevitably comes to mind is the last page of *Phenomenology of Spirit*, with its (modified) citation from Schiller: '*Aus dem Kelche dieses Geisterreiches schäumt ihm seine Unendlichkeit* [From the chalice of this realm of spirits foams forth for Him his own infinitude].' . . . The *Phenomenology*'s last word is a foaming forth, not from 'Him' but from his chalice. There is a totality here, but a totality that proves the totality is not at all a closed totality, but rather one that foams forth to itself as its own infinity" (*German Philosophy*, 22).

23. As Nancy writes in one of his dialogues with Philippe Lacoue-Labarthe, "What is indestructible is fragility itself, more attenuated, more tremulous, more untenable, unbearable, than any fragmentation, the fragility that dwells in speaking or in writing, in opening your mouth, in tracing a word" (*Expectation*, 133, emphasis in original).

24. Morin, "How Do We Live Here," 113.

25. "In all extremity, not only do the interior, the inside, or the property of a being reach their limit, the ultimate point of their completion and of their closure, but they also exceed this closure and undo their own completion . . . the substantiality of the cogito is finally nothing other than its extremity" (Nancy, *Ego Sum*, 79).

26. Morin, "How Do We Live Here," 112.

27. "What of the resonance of that which arouses desire and fear, a resonance we refer to as 'lyricism.' . . . Poetry cannot not be exposed to an unstable, even inconsistent, limit between speech and music. This means 'song'" (Nancy, *Expectation*, 120).

28. Nancy, *Experience*, 90.

29. Nancy, *Ego Sum*, 107.

30. Nancy, *Experience*, 66, emphasis in original.

31. Ibid., 90, emphasis in original

Scandalous Death

1. This essay was originally published in *Angelaki: Journal of the Theoretical Humanities* 27, issue 1 (February 2022): *After Life: Recent Philosophy and Death*, edited by Rona Cohen and Ruth Ronen, and appears through the kind permission of the journal. [Nancy is referring to the following passage in volume 5 of Proust's *In Search of Lost Time*: They buried him [Bergotte], but all through that night of mourning, in the lighted shop-windows, his books, arranged three by three, kept vigil like angels with outspread wings and seemed, for him who was no more, the symbol of his resurrection. See Marcel Proust, *The Captive, The Fugitive*, trans. C. K. Scott Moncrieff and Terence Kilmartin, rev. D. J. Enright (New York: Random House, 1993), 246.—Trans.]

2. In a relationship, however, that is as evident as it is complex in terms of time and content, with the major spiritual transformations of the East.

3. To what extent, today, does the only philosopher who conceives of an immortality as correlate of an existence relative to a world, an existence that is able to disappear from it in order to reappear in another—Alain Badiou—exceed or not the Spinozist-Hegelian schema (and the Leibnizian, Nietzschean, etc., one as well) of a "hyperexistence"? This is a question that we will have to address separately and in contrast with what Derrida calls "sur-vival."

4. [Nancy is referring to Spinoza, *Ethics*, Book V, Prop XXIII, scholium. The Latin reads "At nihilominus sentimus experimurque nos aeternos esse." In the

English translation by R.H.M. Elwes: "But, notwithstanding, we feel and know that we are eternal."—Trans.]

5. [Nancy is referring to Rimbaud's poem from 1872, "Eternity," which he also quotes from in "On a Divine *Wink*," in *Dis-Enclosure: The Deconstruction of Christianity*, trans. Bettina Bergo, Gabriel Malenfant, and Michael B. Smith (New York: Fordham University Press, 2008), 120.—Trans.]

6. [Arthur Rimbaud, "Beauteous Being," in *Illuminations and Other Prose Poems*, trans. Louise Varese (New York: New Directions, 1957), 27.—Trans.]

7. [Nancy is referring to the following passage in Lacan's "Kant with Sade": "Doubtless, in the eyes of such puppets, the millions of men for whom the pain of existing is the original evidence for the practices of salvation which they establish in their faith in Buddha, must be underdeveloped." See Jacques Lacan, "Kant with Sade," trans. James B. Swenson, *October* 51 (1989): 55–75, here 64.—Trans.]

8. [Charles Baudelaire, "The Voyage," in *The Poems and Prose Poems of Charles Baudelaire*, ed. James Huneker (New York: Brentano's, 1919).—Trans.]

Jean-Luc Nancy (1940–2021) was Distinguished Professor of Philosophy at the Université Marc Bloch, Strasbourg. His wide-ranging thought runs through many books, including *The Literary Absolute, Being Singular Plural, The Ground of the Image, Listening, Corpus, The Disavowed Community,* and *Sexistence.*

Jeff Fort is Associate Professor of French at the University of California, Davis, and the translator of more than a dozen books, by Jean Genet, Jacques Derrida, Maurice Blanchot, Jean-Luc Nancy, and others.

Perspectives in Continental Philosophy
John D. Caputo, series editor

Recent titles

Irving Goh, ed., *Jean-Luc Nancy among the Philosophers.*
Jean-Luc Nancy, *Corpus III: Cruor and Other Writings.* Translated by Jeff Fort and Others.
Neal DeRoo, *The Political Logic of Experience: Expression in Phenomenology.*
Marika Rose, *A Theology of Failure: Žižek against Christian Innocence.*
Emmanuel Falque, *The Guide to Gethsemane: Anxiety, Suffering, and Death.* Translated by George Hughes.
Emmanuel Alloa, *Resistance of the Sensible World: An Introduction to Merleau-Ponty.* Translated by Jane Marie Todd. Foreword by Renaud Barbaras.
Françoise Dastur, *Questions of Phenomenology: Language, Alterity, Temporality, Finitude.* Translated by Robert Vallier.
Jean-Luc Marion, *Believing in Order to See: On the Rationality of Revelation and the Irrationality of Some Believers.* Translated by Christina M. Gschwandtner.
Adam Y. Wells, ed., *Phenomenologies of Scripture.*
An Yountae, *The Decolonial Abyss: Mysticism and Cosmopolitics from the Ruins.*
Jean Wahl, *Transcendence and the Concrete: Selected Writings.* Edited and with an Introduction by Alan D. Schrift and Ian Alexander Moore.
Colby Dickinson, *Words Fail: Theology, Poetry, and the Challenge of Representation.*
Emmanuel Falque, *The Wedding Feast of the Lamb: Eros, the Body, and the Eucharist.* Translated by George Hughes.
Emmanuel Falque, *Crossing the Rubicon: The Borderlands of Philosophy and Theology.* Translated by Reuben Shank. Introduction by Matthew Farley.
Colby Dickinson and Stéphane Symons (eds.), *Walter Benjamin and Theology.*
Don Ihde, *Husserl's Missing Technologies.*
William S. Allen, *Aesthetics of Negativity: Blanchot, Adorno, and Autonomy.*
Jeremy Biles and Kent L. Brintnall, eds., *Georges Bataille and the Study of Religion.*
Tarek R. Dika and W. Chris Hackett, *Quiet Powers of the Possible: Interviews in Contemporary French Phenomenology.* Foreword by Richard Kearney.
Richard Kearney and Brian Treanor, eds., *Carnal Hermeneutics.*

A complete list of titles is available at www.fordhampress.com.

www.ingramcontent.com/pod-product-compliance
Lightning Source LLC
Chambersburg PA
CBHW060453080526
44584CB00015B/1419